# Kirstie's Homemade Home

For Ben and the boys,
Orion, Hal, Bay and Oscar –
you make my home.

# Kirstie's Homemade Home

## Kirstie Allsopp

Edited by Lisa McCann

HODDER &
STOUGHTON

# Contents

This book is not just about me or my home. I want it to be an inspiration, a useful tool and a pick-me-up for other people in their homes too. I want everyone to be able to find something in here that they want to make or buy or collect or give to someone they love, even if it's only the book itself.

Life is not always easy, but on TV we are rather inclined to make it look that way, so when you watch a show like *Kirstie's Homemade Home* it can all pass in a flurry of needles, glue and soldering irons. In this book we have pinned down the techniques, hints and fun bits, and put everything you need to know on a permanent page with gorgeous pictures to linger over. There are more than 25 fantastic projects to make, and tons of creative ideas to inspire. So whether you fancy making your own teacup candles, quilting, knitting, flower arranging, rag-rugging or decorating your cakes with edible glitter – believe me when I say that it's just as much fun to decorate cakes as it is to eat them! – I guarantee you'll find something to get stuck into.

But first things first; the inspiration for the TV series and this book was originally Meadowgate, a house I bought in north Devon that had been lying empty for almost four decades. When I look at it today, with its white walls and pretty blue windows, the dilapidated state in which I found the house seems like such a distant memory. But don't be fooled. Renovating a house is incredibly hard work and what began for me in a moment of joy at auction turned into... well, let's call it a labour of love.

But the renovation work aside, what really excited me about Meadowgate was that it presented the ultimate blank canvas. With five bedrooms, two bathrooms, a grown-up sitting room, a playroom for the kids, and a fantastic family kitchen that works as the hub of the home, it was the perfect house for me to create my own dream interior. It also allowed me to share the things I love about good old-fashioned British style through my passion for handmade things and my love of second-hand furnishings that can be found in markets, auctions, reclamation yards and antiques shops up and down the country.

I'm in and out of houses all the time and I wanted to use my experience to make a stand against the flatpack, 'identikit' invasion and throw-away mentality I see everywhere. There's tons of lovely stuff at car boot sales, salvage yards and antiques markets, all of it just waiting for its potential to be recognised and snapped up. This book is proof of that.

More than anything, I hope these pages contribute something to the crafting lexicon. It is about a journey into a world full of dedicated and talented people who make beautiful things, both traditional and modern. Their commitment to the wonderful crafting heritage we have in the UK is proof that handmade British things are here to stay.

I've learnt so much during my years of working in property, but never have I had so much fun as being taught the amazing skills and getting insights into the passions of the craftspeople featured in this book – from Dean Agate, who showed me it was possible to bend iron and make my own poker, to Jo Colwill, who helped me make a truly beautiful quilt for my first son that will last generations. And from Suzie Johnson, who proved to me that I could knit, even though I'm left-handed, to Hilary Charlesworth, whose passion and skill for spinning and weaving has been going strong for more than 27 years. These are but a few of the people and crafts you will meet in the pages that follow.

If you enjoyed the TV shows, you'll see that this book both builds on and branches out from them, and I hope that approach will continue to grow and flourish. If you didn't see any of the series, then welcome to my world. This is what I think is pretty, fun for the whole family and hugely informative. It's a book for mothers and daughters, and (trust me) sons. There is nothing more manly than blacksmithing or glassblowing. If you're looking for a new hobby, or you just want a moment to yourself and something lovely to look at, this book will not disappoint.

I was not the 'arty one' at school, far from it, but my experiences are proof that anyone can have a go at crafts, that if you thought you weren't 'clever with your hands' then you're wrong, you just haven't met the right teacher. In these pages are the pictures, words and guiding hands of so many people to whom I am eternally grateful. They let me into their world and taught me so much. I hope all of you will give at least one thing in this book a try, and I'm absolutely certain that you'll feel as chuffed to bits with the results as I did.

Welcome to the amazing world of crafts: once you've entered, there's no going back.

# Room by room

# Your dream home

It's my theory that in order to make your house a dream home, you need to fill it with things you love and that you'll treasure for years to come, not the cheap imported goods that we constantly throw out and replace. Meadowgate was my way of tempting other people to try a different approach to interior decorating.

I don't profess to be an expert on interior design, but more than a decade of looking at houses while working on *Location, Location, Location* and *Relocation, Relocation*, plus my time at *Country Living* magazine, as well as growing up surrounded by people who work in the worlds of antiques and interiors, has definitely had its effects on me. I'm a self-confessed addict of making, buying, keeping and collecting things that I love for my home. Most importantly, I've learnt to be confident about my taste, which may be different from my friends', my mum's, or even yours – the point is, it's my taste and what I like. That's what the following pages are about. As well as offering hints and tips to spark ideas, I want to empower and give you the confidence to start injecting some of your own unique style into each room of your house so that you can create your own dream interior too.

# The  kitchen

We all have little rules that we follow when it comes to clothes, and in my opinion, interiors are exactly the same. When it comes to the kitchen, I have a rule of three, meaning that I go with a theme of three 'fitted' things. At Meadowgate I opted for very plain white units and tiles, a neutral surface of wooden worktops, and a cream Aga. Those three things formed the basis for my kitchen, and from there I could build and accessorise, adding my lovely blue fridge, which I absolutely adore, and a blue and white theme with my crockery.

My rules are not rigid – think of them more as manners that help you decide what to do in every situation. For example, in my kitchen the decor is simply about trying *not* to make everything look too crazy. And when it comes to accessorising, it pays to be a bit prudent too. Decisions need to be made on such subjects as whether you want your foodstuffs or fancy cooking utensils to double up as decoration, or whether, like me, your life is too chaotic to keep the ketchup bottle clean. I live with five boys, and it's impossible to avoid chaos in my kitchen, so I prefer to have those things hidden away.

You definitely want your kitchen to last you around 10–15 years, if not longer. But over that time your life is very likely to change in that your taste will alter, fashions will come and go, you'll break six plates and change dinner sets, you might start a family, or the children will grow up and fly the nest. So when choosing those 'fitted' things, think about longevity in style as well as practicality, and also how you might alter their look five years down the line. In this way you can refresh, revamp and fall back in love with that space without it costing an arm and a leg.

## Storage

When deciding what you want in your kitchen, think about your priorities and how you want the room to work for you. Storage is key, and having as many places to dump things as possible will save your sanity. I'm also a huge fan of those large pan drawers, whereas my other half has a wide selection of old butcher's racks that he hangs from the ceiling in every house he develops or we live in. I loathe the blooming things! Pans can never be clean enough in my opinion, which is why, for me, pan drawers are up there with penicillin as one of the greatest inventions of the twentieth century. But many people side with him and love to have things hanging and on view.

At present, from the butcher's rack in our London home, there hangs a butterfly, an aeroplane, two sieves, a couple of pans, a filthy toast rack and a fish made of recycled flip flops that my mother brought back from Africa. Does this tell you that I'm not the boss in my own home? I did, however, put my foot down at Meadowgate.

## Worktops and surfaces

In a busy kitchen there must be plenty of workspace and easy access to everything. But in order to keep things convenient and to free up precious worktops, you need a couple of strong shelves for the things you use most. For example, I have a special-edition pink Kitchen Aid blender that I bought at a breast cancer charity auction (hence the pink). It's brilliant but weighs a ton, so however my kitchen is designed, there has to be an easily accessible place to stash it with a socket near by. I also have a small bowl and mini whisk that I use every single day for beating eggs for omelettes, French toast, pancake batter and suchlike for the children. I always want that bowl within easy reach, so my kitchen will always have a small shelf by the cooker for these little things I use all the time. And the same goes for all other kitchen essentials you might have. Kitchens should be fun and stress-free, and my best advice is to think really hard about how *you* run *your* kitchen and plan its design from there.

My preferred worktop is wood – it looks good and doesn't date. You can combine it with other surfaces too. For example, wood goes beautifully with slate, and I like a wooden chopping area on each side of my cooker where I can put trivets for resting hot things. Worktops can be expensive, but to ensure they won't date and that you get your money's worth, always err on the side of simplicity when it comes to colour.

## Cookers

For me, kitchens are all about food and entertaining, but that doesn't mean we're all cooks. So whatever cooker you decide to put in your kitchen, think with your purse as well as your head. Consider which one best suits you in a practical sense, as well as suiting your aesthetic sensitivities. There are lots of cooker options out there, such as ranges, slot-in cookers, built-in hobs – the choice is yours. I'm a proud Aga owner, but I'm well aware they're a bit like Marmite: you either love them or hate them. I'm actually a convert. I wasn't brought up with Agas as my mum loathes them.

You will get sick of me saying this (and I will repeatedly say it throughout this book), but research is where the Internet comes into its own. You can price-check, shop around, look for second-hand (you can buy reconditioned Agas) – basically, you'll find the greatest variety possible online. And then you can go off and find a local supplier and suss it out in the flesh.

## Displays and dressers

Ever since I worked at *Country Living* magazine when I was 19 years old, I have wanted a dresser. And hard as it might be to believe, and I shan't tell you how many years have passed, my first dresser was the one I bought for Meadowgate. I love it.

It's got to be admitted that the dresser is probably not the most practical way of storing your crockery, and if you're pushed for space in your kitchen, don't even think about it! But every single week in every auction I go to, I see dressers galore that are going for a song: the one I bought cost £200. If you don't have the space, there are alternative ways to get the same pretty display effect. Try buying shelving units, either old or new, and putting them above your more modern kitchen cupboards or pan drawers. Dressers and shelves are a really good way of combining the pleasure of displaying your pretty crockery with a practical space-saving option.

**PREVIOUS SPREAD:**
The fabulous dresser in my friend Sasha Schwerdt's house.

Traditionally, dressers were purely functional, used just for storing crockery and kitchenware, and that's still their primary role today. But they've also become very fashionable pieces. In a family environment, where space is precious, some would say that a dresser is a dumping ground for all sorts of stuff, but I think it's a fantastically hard-working piece of furniture.

## Tables and chairs

A kitchen table is a flat piece of wood with four legs. Do not forget that. If you have a limited budget for your kitchen, you cannot afford to splash out on an overly expensive piece of furniture like a table. And you don't have to. One of the best things about shopping for second-hand furniture is that it can be very cheap – our kitchen table in London is a case in point. Although that said, this particular table has a very uneven surface that is a pain in the bum because the children are constantly knocking over cups of juice that aren't balanced properly. So think practically as well as with your purse strings.

I like to talk across the table, so I prefer a long, narrow shape, but obviously your table depends on the space you have available. If you're looking to buy an old table and you see one in an antiques shop, make sure that the legs are arranged in such a way that you can maximise the space underneath. Unless the table is actually an original Chippendale or suchlike, it's not an act of vandalism to take a good sturdy tabletop and put it on different legs. People have been doing it for hundreds of years. Wood lasts a very long time and, if you ask me, it's better to buy an old table and adapt it than to buy a new one.

When it comes to seating, I am a great believer in the banquette. If you have limited space in the kitchen, there is no point having a table in the middle of your room and then trying to squeeze chairs and people around it. I think it's a great idea to put a square or circular table in the corner of the room, 1980s' style, and have built-in bench seats in that corner, which accommodate far more people and take up far less space. And if they have lift-up seats, you get a load of storage to boot. People don't think of banquettes any more – you probably all think I'm raving mad suggesting them now. But I swear, they're fantastic.

The kitchen at Meadowgate has benches around the table simply because you can fit more people on them. What's also great is that my two benches worked out way cheaper than if I'd bought eight or ten chairs. They were old school benches that I picked up at my local antiques warehouse, Fagin's in Devon. It turned out they were actually a bit low for the table, and really I should have measured the correct height I needed bums to sit at. Never mind, one day I will get round to building them up with blocks underneath the feet. But since I got the pair for £150, I don't mind them being a little bit low in the short term.

## Crocks and pots

Britain has an extraordinary history of ceramic design and was once one of the largest global exporters of ceramic tableware in the world. Household names such as Wedgwood and Spode earned their reputation producing tea sets and dinner services like the type you'll remember your granny using when you were little. Sadly, what was once a thriving ceramic industry has perished, but there are still numerous small, independent potters out there making beautiful things in workshops all over the UK, and they need our support.

I was introduced to Steve Harrison, a potter for 24 years, who can craft anything from clay, but who specialises in making teapots and cups. A word about Steve – the man lives for throwing pots. Honestly, I've never met anyone like him – he is truly potty. But the results of his immeasurable passion for the craft are nothing short of breathtaking.

While I loved watching Steve throw in the studio he built in his back garden, it did make me shy to have a go myself – I had a sneaking feeling my own performance wouldn't be so convincing. However, the idea of creating something myself was exciting, and everything I learnt at school came flooding back to me the moment the clay started spinning between my hands. With some guidance and coaching from Steve, I managed to keep it steady (just) and make a simple little bowl. I became completely attached to it (you get like that with things you've made yourself), so when Steve said I had to leave it with him so he could take it to be fired in his kiln in Wales, I was worried. The thing with firing pots is that some don't survive the process. And one-fifth of all the pots

Steve fires don't make it... But mine did survive and now sits proudly on the kitchen dresser at Meadowgate.

It's wonderful to imagine your dresser displaying a collection of chipped and loved family bits collected over the years, but that's a dream scenario. I started from scratch with the crockery on the dresser at Meadowgate. It's a mixture of new pieces from potters I love – Steve; Nicholas Mosse, whose pottery in Ireland I've visited often; and the constantly irresistible Brixton Pottery wares – plus old stuff bought at auction and in various antiques shops. My point is that we all have to start somewhere, and an heirloom can start life tomorrow, in your home, on your shelf or dresser.

# The sitting room

If you're looking for ultra-modern design ideas, you've probably already realised that you're reading the wrong book, and the sitting room is perhaps the room where I am most conventional. I like old-fashioned, comfy sofas, pictures on walls, a bookshelf or desk, and definitely a coffee table or pouffe of some sort that can double up as a useful surface and an additional seat.

What you do with your sitting room depends entirely on how many other rooms you have in your house and whether or not you have young children. The London flat I live in has been under construction in some way or another for more than two years. (Yes, it drives me nuts!) So despite the fact that one day the children *will* have a playroom, at the moment we cook, eat, sit and they play in the one room. Including my stepchildren, I have four boys between the ages of one and ten, so there's a lot of plastic with wheels or wings around the place! And if a similar scenario is played out in your home, make sure that your sitting room is just as hard-working as the kitchen and is able to put up as good a fight.

At Meadowgate, however, the sitting room was always going to be an adult room, and it was an enormous luxury being able to do it up as such. It doesn't even have a television. It is a proper grown-up drawing room.

As I'm writing this, my 18-month-old son is entertaining himself with my button box. Sewing equipment is one of the things I've always kept in the sitting room. I like large pieces of old furniture, but so often the drawers and cupboards in our sitting rooms have nothing in them. What do you store in the sitting room? Allocating that space to things that have no real home is a good idea. Sitting-room cupboards usually house a selection of unused board games, the odd, almost finished scented candle, and a couple of unopened or undelivered Christmas presents. (I always feel like I've lucked out when I discover the still-wrapped chocolates.) But seriously, at the risk of sounding patronising, use the storage available to you in that room. You'd be amazed by the number of people who don't.

## Flooring and rugs

Now that I can afford it, my preferred flooring downstairs is wood. That said, there are some really good-quality laminates on the market these days, much better than the awful yellow springy stuff that was on the floor in my first flat. The important thing to consider is your budget. Be it carpets, wood, tiles or whatever you decide to have underfoot, use your head and think about durability as well as aesthetics. The flooring in a room is perhaps the most irreversible outlay and it requires a good deal of thought.

If you opt for a hard floor, you'll probably want a rug of some sort too – a collection of different rugs also works really well. I'll admit that before *Homemade Home*, I knew nothing about the cost, quality or value of rugs, and I've never had any luck finding cheap, second-hand ones, so my ethos of reusing or recycling was really put to the test when buying rugs. On a couple of occasions, my other half has brought home lovely second-hand rugs, but his purchases have caused moth infestations in our house. (If you do find good stuff second-hand, I'd definitely advise de-mothing and airing before you allow it indoors.) Then I started thinking about rugs for Meadowgate and met Hilary Charlesworth, and suddenly buying new looked like an interesting option.

Hilary is a spinner and weaver of tapestries and rugs. She's the real deal, an artisan who adores her craft and has been developing it for more than 27 years. And you'd have to love it, because like so many of the crafts I've tried for *Kirstie's Homemade Home*, these artists aren't in it for the money. Hilary makes absolutely beautiful rugs that she sells from as little as £150. I know that's not peanuts, but when you consider that it takes her a week to make one rug, you soon realise that she's working for well below the minimum wage.

Hilary works with a traditional hand spinning-wheel, drawing out the fibre of the wool with her hands and treading the wheel with her foot. The wheel does the work of twisting the wool into yarn, but it's not as easy as it looks. It's like patting your head and rubbing your stomach at the same time, which I've never been able to master. I spent the entire time looking as though I was catching flies, mouth wide open, trying to concentrate. It was a real eye-opener to the skill involved in this craft. Of course, there are modern-day spinning-wheels and electric machines that mass-produce in a fraction of the time, but where is the romance in that? Hilary was able to take my large bag of wool (from my own Manx sheep) and use it to make something wonderful with her own two hands. And for me, that's magical.

If you're looking for a new rug, remember the Hilarys of the UK (the few that are left, that is), consider their prices and the work they are doing. You can shop online, or in select stores, and buy something truly unique. I took one of Hilary's beautiful handmade rugs home, and I smile every time I see it.

All this rug talk refers to large rugs; see page 42 for my thoughts on bedroom rugs.

# Lighting

Sitting rooms require a variety of different lights – lights for reading, lights for relaxing and lights for entertaining. There are whole books dedicated to how to light a room. I'm not a specialist in the subject, but for me lighting, or at least lamps and lampshades, are about what you like and what you don't. I'm a fan of traditional lighting, i.e. lamps, dotted around the room, partly because you can adjust the level of light so easily.

Lighting is a vital element of interior decor, yet when I'm looking at houses up and down the country, it is surprisingly rare to walk into a room that has more than one lamp in it. This may be because of the expense and people's fear of getting it wrong, particularly with lampshades, which can happen.

When I was doing the sitting room and bedrooms at Meadowgate I needed lots of lamps for them, but I wanted to avoid it costing an arm and a leg. So I took my favourite lamp base to Eileen Garsed, who makes bespoke lampshades from a small workshop she's created in her house near Bristol. She showed me that, with a bit of effort, it was possible to make my own lampshade in just a few hours, and the result is really fantastic (see page 138 to do it yourself). If you don't have the time to have a go on your own, there are plenty of people out there, like Eileen, who'd be happy and willing to do it for you – and you'll get exactly what you want.

It's worth a trip to your local charity shop if you're looking for lamp bases and shades, although not all charity shops sell electrical goods. People are constantly trading them in, and charity shops (when they do stock them) tend to give these things away for a song. Just check that the wiring is sound before you use them.

If you're doing a room from scratch and having overhead lighting put in, don't overdo it. The number of rooms I see with eight down-lighters when four would suffice is extraordinary. Remember, brightness can be overwhelming, even stressful if you want to relax, so dimmer switches are a good idea to create a calm and welcoming ambience. (Note that standard dimmer switches don't work with energy-saving lightbulbs, so make sure you install those that do.)

While working on the TV series I came across a simple but very effective form of lighting – namely, recycled Kilner jars converted into cool hanging lights. They look great over a dining table, in a bedroom, or anywhere you want to hang them. The point is to look at everything with an eye for purpose. As much as possible, reuse and adapt the things you already have; paint them, transform them, change their use, and move them around your home. It's a great way of recycling and saving money, and – even better – a way of falling back in love with things you've grown a bit tired of.

To see some fantastic ideas for lights, look at the websites of Vaughan Designs and Baileys Home & Garden (see pages 211 and 214).

# Soft furnishings

It is my view that you cannot apply the modern-day goal of immediate gratification to decorating – the rooms that you see in magazines and big stores are not something you should just run out and duplicate. Remember, you have your own tastes and your own sense of style, so use the images you see to give you ideas and create something that *you* love. You want your sitting room to be built up in layers of things you like, things you've been hoarding or collecting for a while, or things that you've been desperate to buy and have saved up for. If you do it in too much of a rush, you'll regret it. The best-dressed rooms and prettiest interiors I've seen have not come together overnight. Patience and forethought are the keys to interior decorating.

When I did my sitting room at Meadowgate, I started off knowing which fabric I wanted for my curtains (as I'm so obsessed with fabric, of course it was the first thing I chose). And to a certain extent, this dictated the choices I made in the rest of the room. I was very pleased when a tartan chair we already had looked surprisingly good with the reddish-pink in the pineapple print of the curtains. I then went for a similarly bright fabric on one sofa, and a plain, neutral fabric on the other. That meant I was sticking to my three-colour rule in the sitting room: the reddish-pink on the curtains and sofa, cream on the other sofa and the tartan chair.

I then added some cushions. Cushions are amazing. They are both comfortable and decorative and you can go on making them, collecting them, using them, washing them... forever. I had one made from an old knitted jumper, a couple from some fabric I had left over from a previously upholstered sofa, some tartan ones to match the tartan chair, and some plain colours to match the other sofa. Re-reading this, it sounds hideous! And you might think it looks hideous... but somehow, the combination works for me and I absolutely love that room.

Cushions can completely alter the look of your sofa/chair/room, and are an easy and inexpensive way to do so when money for bigger changes is tight. My favourite cushion covers are made of linen and cotton because they're washable and can make an old or plain-coloured sofa look a lot more chic. (If you fancy making some yourself, see pages 104 and 167.)

I also adore fabric samples, particularly the large ones that you pay a deposit for. My advice is *always* to get fabric samples. Take them home and drape them over existing sofas and pin them up at windows to get a sense of how they will look in situ. Mistakes can be infuriating and very expensive, so don't rush into making decisions about curtain and upholstery fabrics without thinking about the room as a whole.

Not long ago I had dinner with some friends who had been in their house a year. I thought the place looked wonderful and told them so. My hostess promptly pointed out that she had no fabric on the window seat, but I hadn't noticed that. My eyes took in the bigger picture, and I thought that house was lovely, even if it was unfinished. My point is, don't panic if you can't do it all at once. When we were doing Meadowgate the whole project was being filmed for TV, so getting the house done was my *job*, but believe me, there is still a lot left to do in that house. I didn't feel, and I still don't, that it's finished. I see things I want to buy all the time, and there are constant changes I want to make. You'll probably feel this too about your own home, but getting it right is always better than doing it fast.

# Sofas

Deciding whether to buy new or old sofas depends on two things: personal preference and price. Often, if you buy a new sofa from a furniture shop and have it covered with one of their fabrics, it will in fact be cheaper than buying an old one from, say, an auction house or second-hand shop and re-covering it. But this rule usually applies to 'fashion trend' sofas, the ones many of us tend to replace after a short period of time, rather than the more traditional, classic designs that are expensive when brand new and remain so because they're timeless.

If you're after a more classic design, or just a traditional comfy sofa, my advice is to check out your local auction house and see what's on offer. If you find something you like that's comfortable and in good shape, consider buying it and either have it reupholstered or have loose covers made. I always go for classically designed, comfortable rough-and-tumble sofas, the cheaper the better, though I always make sure the 'carcass' is sound. You can pick up sofas at auction from as little as £150.

If you have young children, loose covers are the answer. They are a bit more expensive, but there is nothing more frustrating than seeing a chocolate-covered paw or a red pen wreck a new or recently upholstered sofa or chair. When having loose covers made, you must not assume that the person making them knows you intend to wash them. It's your responsibility to ensure the fabric you choose is washable.

## Shelving

To my mind, a room isn't properly furnished if it doesn't contain books. I'm always buying them, and I'm always looking for places to put them. I like them to be in view, and preferably where others can take advantage of them. Second-hand bookshelves and bookcases can be picked up easily and cheaply in antiques shops, on the Internet or at auction, and even a couple of cheap shelves will do the trick if you're handy with wall plugs and a screwdriver.

If you like buying and collecting books as much as I do, you might need to be inventive when it comes to storing them. A clever space to use is above doorways and around a room at picture-rail height. You don't need massively high ceilings to do this; a foot or two above the rail is ample. Putting simple white shelving around the top of a room and arranging books on it can be both tidy and really attractive – especially if you've got books with pretty bindings. And even if you haven't, you can find books like this in all sorts of places – charity shops, jumble sales, second-hand book shops. They won't cost much, and even if you don't want to read them, the effect is lovely.

## Fireplaces and surrounds

When I was expecting my second son, my other half dragged me to
a fireplace shop to show me the biggest stone fireplace I've ever seen.
He said he wanted it in our sitting room in London. I saw no other option
but to go down the worst, most manipulative, feminine route. So I burst
into tears and said there was no way I could live with that fireplace.
Three days later I felt guilty, so I said to him, you can buy the fireplace
and you can keep it in storage, and when you find the right place for it,
i.e. in one of your developments, you can put it there – just not in our
sitting room. Five months later, after giving birth to our son and
spending eight weeks in Devon, I returned to London to see our newly
finished flat and there was the fireplace, in our sitting room. Every day
I think one of the children is going to do himself untold damage by
tripping over and cracking his head on that monstrous stone edifice

that we have at the heart of our home. But so far, it hasn't happened. And do I like it? I think this tale probably illustrates that you can get used to anything!

If you buy a house and you don't like the fireplaces, it is OK to change them, unless the property is listed and then you shouldn't. But please, do a bit of research first and if it's an original fireplace, think twice. If you just can't get used to it, consider putting a pretty screen or something in front of it. I did choose to remove all the downstairs fireplaces at Meadowgate. I just didn't feel they were in keeping with the house, and I didn't like them. I was confident I could replace them with something much more fitting that I did like. In the kitchen there is now a Georgian-style surround that I got from Ray Cullop – a salvage-yard owner we visited in north London (see page 217). The other fireplace is in the sitting room, with a surround made from old stone we already had, my hand-crafted poker (made with the help of Dean Agate), and a lovely fire basket I bought at Ray's and then restored. I decided to keep the upstairs fireplaces as they were; after bringing them back to life, I absolutely adore them.

I use my fireplace as a family trophy cabinet – it's full of lots of little mementos and things we've collected. A friend of mine has four large grey stones on her mantelpiece, each of which has the initials of one of her children written on it. This is such a simple thing, but it looks really lovely – an idea well worth copying.

## Televisions

Men, please note – not having a fireplace in your sitting room is no excuse for having your TV at the centre of it instead. Ladies, do not allow this to happen in your home.

Throughout my childhood, our only television was housed under a cloth-draped table, which meant that if we wanted to watch our favourite programmes, we had to go under the table! The TV was flat on the floor too, so you couldn't even watch it from the sofa. My mum is a purist and that was her way of disguising the set. The best thing about modern flat-screen televisions is that they stop the TV dominating the layout of a room.

# Bedrooms

Bedrooms are for sleeping, and every book you read on good health and good sleep will tell you that (a) you should not have a TV in your bedroom, (b) you shouldn't have a computer, and (c) it's not the place to have a telephone or a charging mobile phone. I'm sure all of this is true, but I've always been fortunate enough to fall asleep the second my head hits the pillow, and often before, so I tend not to worry too much about what might be preventing me sleeping. As the child of an insomniac, though, I know how very, very difficult and debilitating lack of sleep can be. So if you can manage it, make your bedroom a proper place of rest.

I didn't have a TV in my room (I must remember to call it *our* room – I lived alone until I was 33, and still have a tendency to refer to it as *my* bedroom, and my other half is forever telling me off) until I was very, very ill with morning sickness with my second child and literally couldn't leave my bed for two months. I got a TV in my room out of necessity and I haven't managed to get it out again because I have become a news junkie. Working all day and not managing to watch the news kills me. It's become a bit of a naughty habit to stay up late and watch it in bed. My advice is, don't bring the TV into your bedroom. Ever. But on the plus side, I don't have a phone in the room, and I don't keep my laptop in there either.

When decorating a bedroom, I like to choose a theme based around the one thing I can't live without, or the one thing I really, really want to have in that room. For example, if you have a favourite set of sheets, a dressing table, or some fabric you really like, use that as the centrepiece for your room and build from there. The style of a lot of the bedrooms at Meadowgate was dictated by the fabrics that I wanted in the rooms. The master bedroom was all about the flowery bedhead my mum gave me; the children's room was built around some green 'Goat Herder' curtains, and one of the other bedrooms was built around an amazing antique American quilt I found. From there, a lot of the decor was easy.

## Beds and quilts

It's well known that we spend a third of our life in bed, so it's really
important to make it comfortable and inviting. One of the best ways
to do this, I reckon, is to add a quilt. I think my passion for quilts came
across on the show when I met quilter Jo Colwill. I've been buying quilts
ever since I had any money. In fact, anything bed-related has always
been an obsession of mine. As a child I longed for a four-poster bed and
eventually I got one – it was dressed with white fabric with green bows
and a pink trim. It was truly the most beautiful bed in the entire world,
but when we moved house my mum had the curtains of my beloved
bed made into blinds for my new room. Why? Because I moved into
the attic...

If you're lucky enough to find quilts that fit over your bed, fantastic. But antique quilts are often antique sizes, sometimes too small to cover a whole bed, and sometimes too precious. But this makes them ideal wall hangings for behind a bed, or you can use a gentle tacking stitch to attach them to an existing bedhead, although bear in mind that over time the exposed part will fade and the wall side will not. In our house we have upholstered bedheads, wall hangings, old bits of panelling and, in some cases, nothing behind the beds at all. It all goes to prove that you can use a variety of things at the head of the bed, and by having bedheads that have a degree of flexibility in their colour and style, you can easily move them around and change the look of a room.

Bed linen is another fixation of mine, and I was recently offered the opportunity to design my own range of sheets. I'm not exaggerating when I say it felt like I'd won the lottery. Over time, as with everything else I buy, I've developed a trick of mixing and matching bedding. If, like me, you like to buy old linen duvets and pillowcases, you have to accept that it's very unlikely you'll get them as a set. But that doesn't mean you shouldn't buy them. I think it's best to mix and match them and just get as much pleasure out of them as you can while they're usable.

## Mattresses

I've said this so many times that I'm sure everyone is bored with hearing it by now, but if you look at the amount of time you spend in your car and the amount of time you spend in your bed and the money spent on each one, the two figures are definitely out of whack. Spending money on a good bed or, in fact, a good mattress, is absolutely *essential*. We did once buy a bed that was too soft, and it was an expensive mistake. My advice to avoid such a costly error is to take the advice of people in bed stores. I love the Internet, but while you can order a bed online, you cannot test it, so this is definitely a case of try before you buy.

I buy my beds from Vi-Spring because they're brilliant and they're made in England (see page 214). In fact, mattress-making is a real craft and its exponents deserve to be supported, so think hard about where you're getting yours from.

# Bedroom rugs

Rugs that warm toes when they come out of bed in the morning are wonderful; wooden or hard flooring first thing on a winter's morn is not. So if you have wooden floors, as we do at Meadowgate and at home in east Devon, it's really nice to have something soft underfoot next to the bed. It also breaks up the expanse of floor.

My favourite bedroom rugs are sheepskins, but they vary in price enormously. The cheapest I've found come from the Fenland Sheepskin Company in Somerset (see page 216), and their small ones are perfect for stepping onto when you hop out of bed. Despite looking all creamy and delicate, they're actually very resilient, as I discovered when my dog was sick on one just 24 hours after it arrived at Meadowgate. I hung the rug outside, gave it a shower with the hose and put it on the airer over the Aga. The next day it looked like new.

For the second series of *Homemade Home* I got to make a rag rug. I've wanted to make one ever since my friend Isobel gave me one as a present, which I absolutely adore. That one is quite plain, which is unusual for a rag rug, but it's in a heart shape and is in my bathroom. The rug I made with textile artist Debbie Siniska is more traditional, a repeated leaf pattern in lots of zingy colours (see page 158 if you'd like to have a go at making it yourself).

God knows, I've got enough odds and sods of cloth to make rag rugs for the rest of my life; in fact, making a rag rug is one of my great justifications for never throwing anything away!

## Walls

Given half a chance I would wallpaper every wall of every room in every house I see. I have a genuine love for wallpaper, but I have to admit I've never been a great fan of the 'feature wall', or covering only one wall with wallpaper.

The idea of wallpaper, or covering walls with a repeated pattern, first came about over 500 years ago, with original designs being hand-painted or stencilled to imitate the styles, patterns and textures of fabrics or wall coverings that would have been fashionable at the time. It wasn't until the 1800s, when a Lancashire firm developed a machine to make the first manufactured wallpaper, that the product became affordable for everyone. Nowadays the selection available is vast – florals, of course, but also stripes, spots and abstracts, from monochrome to multicoloured, and there's even interactive-designed wallpaper on the market. It's a joy.

The kitsch, eccentric and ironic are all characteristics of personal taste, and it pays to be bold these days – it's all about statements and being brave enough to do something you love.

But handmade wallpaper is certainly not a budget item, with many designs costing more than £100 a roll. Do the maths before setting your heart on an unaffordable design. Good-quality paint can decorate just as well, and there is a vast array of colours to choose from. (See page 150 if you fancy designing and screen-printing your own wallpaper.)

# Pictures and plates

Interior decorator (and my old boss) Nicky Haslam once said that photographs were fine as long as they were of royals and on the piano. Now, much as I love him, I think he's wrong about this. It's *your* home, and although your guests might not be so fixated by pictures of your children or your favourite moments, *you* are, and that's what matters. For me, family portraits are definitely the oil paintings of our age. One of the best advances in recent years is the lower cost of printing digital photographs. And something I love is a cluster of small pictures and paintings close together on walls.

I grew up surrounded by paintings and I find empty walls a bit of a travesty, if I'm honest. It does take a while to build these things up, and that's why four or five clusters of little postcards or photographs are a great way to start. And remember that you can buy pictures and paintings for a snip in charity shops, auctions, markets and second-hand shops all over the country. It is a time-invested thing and you will have to do a bit of sifting to find something you like. However, photographs are easy. We all have our favourite moments that we want to remember every day, and hanging them on a wall is the best way to do just that.

When I buy a picture, I never worry what it might be worth. If I like it, and can afford to pay what they're asking, I'll buy it. If, as happened one weekend, I find something for £5 that I absolutely love, I'm doubly thrilled. A framed and glazed 1950s'-style print of a painting of some roses for five quid? Now you won't get that in any of your big warehouse stores, will you! Chain stores charge an arm and a leg for mass-produced pictures. I see the same ones in houses up and down the country. Why would you part with your hard-earned cash for something that ubiquitous when you can have a personal memory enlarged and displayed on your wall for a lot less?

You can buy frames in marketplaces everywhere. They're often more valuable than the pictures themselves, but you can buy cheap ones, and it's what you put in the frame that will make it beautiful.

Another inexpensive and very effective way of adding interest to plain walls is to hang plates on them. People often chuck away odd

plates because they don't know what to do with them, so you'll always see stacks of them in reclamation yards and charity shops – unloved and dirty, but just waiting for someone to see their potential as part of their colour scheme. Over the years I've collected tons of prettily patterned china plates for next to nothing and turned them into wall arrangements that look really beautiful – to me at least. As I say, it's all about what you do and don't like, and this is something I love to do.

The traditional way of hanging plates is to use stretchy wire plate hangers, but over time these have a nasty habit of digging into the edges of the china. I've found a fantastic substitute for these: adhesive circles that have a metal loop attached to one edge. You just stick one on the back of the plate and bob's your uncle – an invisible and non-damaging way of displaying your find.

I always think it's better to group plates together rather than hang them individually. A single plate can look a bit forlorn, but several together make a real statement. The fact that they're all different doesn't matter a bit, but it does look great if you can pick up on a particular colour. My mum has some green-themed plates in her hallway hanging just above a green upholstered chair. They cost very little, but the combined effect looks terrific.

# Layout and storage

Some bedrooms are barely big enough to fit a bed, in which case don't fight it; accept that all you'll do in that room is sleep, and get a decent bedhead so at least you can sit up in comfort. If the space permits, you're looking at having a bedside table or two. There's no need for them to be a matching pair – in my bedroom one bedside table is a chest of drawers. Basically, you have to use every corner of space available and maximise its uses.

I am a *huge* fan of pegs for hanging things. I'm driven absolutely bonkers when I stay somewhere I can't hang up my things in view, i.e. hotel rooms. Someone somewhere has two beautiful beige satin dresses that I used as nightgowns and left behind in a hotel wardrobe. Had there been any pegs on the walls, that loss would never have happened. Obviously, I'm not saying that your home is a hotel, but if you have a guest room and there is no space for a wardrobe, or you want to use that space for something else, put in a row of pegs with some hangers behind a door or on a wall. Add a little chest of drawers to double as a table, and that is more than adequate storage for a visitor of a couple of nights.

But peg rails are not just for guest rooms. Consider having pegs in your own room too. Being a mum, I have little time to myself, and on days when I'm filming, I'm in more of a rush than ever, so I like to plan what I'm wearing the night before and have it hanging on pegs, ready for me to put on in the morning.

If your room is big enough, make use of the space at the end of the bed. I keep all my sheets and pillowcases in a blanket box at the end of my bed. But don't put blankets or winter clothes in a blanket box because six months later you'll discover it's alive with moths and everything is ruined! I wish I had a solution to the moth problem. I don't, but I do believe in lavender bags – as many lavender bags as possible. And they are so easy to make yourself (see page 100).

Another piece of furniture I recommend in the bedroom is a dressing table. A friend gave me my dressing table over 15 years ago. It was the first piece of furniture I ever painted, and I can't have done that bad a job because it's still going strong, although occasionally the mirror tips forward and knocks everything down, which is rather annoying. It's on

my list of things to get fixed, but that's a long list! All my hairbrushes, hairdryer, countless sprays and products (part of the endless quest for pre-baby hair) live in a basket underneath my dressing table. It's a sacred space.

I could write an entire book about clothes storage, but there are others who can do that far better than I. All you have to do is Google-image Mariah Carey's dressing room and you'll see exactly what I mean. I'm getting goosebumps just thinking about it.

## Curtains and cushions

I'm a great believer in curtains. In fact, I believe in curtains far more than I believe in double-glazing. A well-made pair of curtains with some heavy interlining will keep the noise and light out, and the warmth in. You can buy second-hand curtains, second-hand fabrics or new fabrics from haberdasheries and curtain-making shops. You can even make your own curtains if you want to save yourself some cash – get a wriggle on with your sewing machine.

I also love cushions. I am a demon fluffer and folder, but I cannot stand piles and piles and piles of cushions on my bed. Why? Because for every one cushion I chuck off the bed, or every dozen that the children throw off in a day, I have to pick them up and put them back in place. If you want cushions on your bed – and they do look lovely – I'm convinced that two large cushions are just as pretty and effective as half a dozen small ones.

**OPPOSITE:**
This fantastic curtain in Sasha Schwerdt's house is made from an old rug. To make it fit without cutting, and thus keep the option of using it as a rug again, the end is simply folded over and rings sewn on the back for the pole. The fold acts like a pelmet that moves with the curtain when it's opened or closed.

# Bathrooms

Without doubt, the greatest luxury in life is not having to share your bathroom with either your partner or your children. Most of the time this is just not possible. But if you do have two bathrooms in your house and you can strike some kind of deal with your children and partner to allow you to keep one bathroom as *your* sacred territory, then go ahead and sell your soul. On an average day as a working mum, I know that this is the only room in the house where I'll get any semblance of peace, usually in the morning, before anyone else is awake.

If you have only one bathroom, it's essential to make it adaptable and as child-friendly as possible. And, as with every other room in the house, try to keep a consistent theme in the decor. The main bathroom at Meadowgate has an old art deco bath that I found in my local antiques warehouse. The moment I saw it, I knew that bath would provide the theme for my bathroom. I wanted it to emulate the old school glamour and luxury that the art deco era captured so well. And for the other bathroom, I went for a child-friendly seaside theme with a good-sized shower box but no bathtub. (For the times the children need a bath, I pop them into the main bathroom.)

The master bedroom at Meadowgate also has a bath in it. The trend for this started in boutique hotels in the early 1990s, but it hasn't really taken hold. Lisa, who produces the TV series of *Homemade Home*, says it's because people don't have the space, but I disagree with that. People are always carving up bedrooms to install en-suite bathrooms when it would be just as easy to put a sink and bath in the corner. I reckon you'd end up with just as much space, if not more. I also think you can put a loo in a cupboard, but family and friends who I've shared this theory with disagree with me entirely. Maybe they're right about that one.

The great thing about bathrooms is that you can go on adding to them and accessorising them forever. In fact, some of the most fabulous designs and interiors I've ever seen are in bathrooms.

# Bathroom fittings

We recently bought a top-of-the-range bath at a fraction of its original cost because it's chipped. In fact, nearly all our baths have some sort of flaw. My point is that many bathroom shops (and, come to think of it, appliance stores in general) will have scratched or damaged products that you can buy for less.

I know that killing the urge to have everything new and pristine is really hard. I'm very tidy, pathologically clean, and it took me a long time to come to terms with buying furniture and fittings that were damaged (and I certainly don't do it all the time). But once you start to become obsessed with buying decorative objects for your home (quilts, cushions, pictures and the like), you need to find the disposable income from somewhere, and suddenly it all adds up. Saving money by opting for a chipped, discounted bath beats a perfect one any day.

**PAGE 52:**
Anouska Hempel's blue bathroom (bottom left) is just perfect; I wouldn't change a thing.

**BELOW RIGHT:**
Burgh Island Hotel in south Devon is an art deco gem, and its bathrooms definitely influenced my choices at Meadowgate.

When we bought our east Devon house the bathrooms were brand new, but we didn't like them. Over time, we've replaced different bits, such as sinks, baths, tiles, taps and so on. They don't all match, and they don't have to. If you're doing a bathroom, it can be a gradual and ongoing process where you change little bits at different times according to what you can afford. I suppose that's where living with older furniture and second-hand stuff is in many ways easier. You get out of the habit of having everything matching, and you realise that it can still look great.

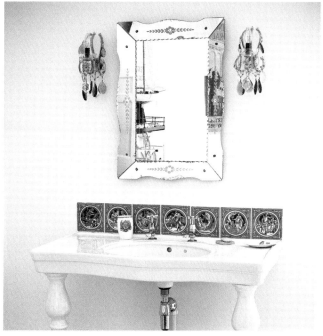

## Tiles

If I can re-tile a bathroom, anybody can – and I do mean that I actually cut and stuck the tiles myself. If, for example, you move into a house with a peach- or avocado-coloured bathroom that makes you feel semi-suicidal every time you look at it, but the purchase price of the house has removed any hope of replacing that suite soon, don't despair. Something as small scale as re-tiling can make a *huge* difference.

Go out and find some antique or second-hand tiles, not expensive ones, which have in them a bit of avocado or peach, or else some colours that complement the 'suicide' suite, then go to a tile wholesaler and buy some plain tiles in a colour that also works with the suite. Buy them as cheaply as you possibly can, and then get tiling. If you have to, replace the taps too – you can pick these up at reclamation yards or bathroom wholesale shops – and suddenly your 'suicide' suite will get a whole new lease of life.

The price differences when it comes to buying tiles are staggering. They range from as little as £5 per square metre to over £75 and upwards. I always shop around for tiles. When buying new ones, I look for ends of lines and for what I can afford. It's very rare to find antique or second-hand tiles in large quantities, so with the small batches I do find, I tend to use them in clusters, such as splashbacks above sinks.

# Shelves

For me, shelves in the bathroom are essential. The gold and marble shelving unit at Meadowgate is, we think, a 1930s'-style plant stand that would have originally been used to decorate a hall or conservatory. Winning that plant stand at auction was a real joy. It cost me £175, and its marble shelves make it ideal for a bathroom. It is a big, solid piece of furniture, and fortunately that bathroom has the space to take it along one of the walls.

Quite recently, on my local Devon high street, I came across a man selling bits and bobs out of the back of a truck, including a really pretty set of wooden bathroom shelves for £20. I bought them and put them aside for future use, but I will find a place for them very soon. Those too were a great find. It's all about seeing an opportunity and making it work for you.

I buy lots of shelves. You can pick up dark wood and scruffy pine shelves a dime a dozen, and repainting them is easy as pie. But if you *are* painting the shelves, remember that many bathroom lotions and potions have ingredients in them that melt paint, so it might be worth investing in some glass to go on top of the shelves to protect them. You can get this cut to fit from your local glazier.

I think bathrooms are fantastic for storage – the bathroom in my old one-bed flat also housed my washing-machine and tumble-dryer. I boxed them into a cupboard, where I also stored any clothes that were out of season or didn't need hanging. Many houses don't have the space for a separate laundry room, especially if you're trying to maximise the size of the kitchen, but if a bathroom is big enough to have a bath and separate shower, you might think of removing the shower and installing a stacked washing-machine and tumble-dryer in that space (do check first, though, about any safety restrictions concerning the use of electricity in bathrooms). Personally, I've never been a fan of the combination of dirty clothes and food that is inevitable if you're doing your laundry in the kitchen.

# The sociable bathroom

I love to socialise in the bathroom. One friend maintains that the best way to corner a man is to do it while he's in the bath – and I think she's probably right. In any case, I'm a firm believer in the bathroom chair. It's somewhere for visitors and clothes to perch, and if you've got children, you're going to get great use out of it. I attach a very high importance to being able to sit down pronto once I've got my child out of the bath. And that's not just because my first child weighed in at 11 lb 11 oz! Baths are also a great way of entertaining the kids, and I'm inclined to leave mine in there until they turn blue and wrinkly, so I need somewhere to sit and watch them.

For obvious reasons, it's not ideal to have an upholstered chair in a bathroom (though I do at Meadowgate – I just try to keep it clear of splashing). A little wooden chair, or one with washable loose covers, is a better bet and can look really nice. Or if you're really struggling for space, get a small stool. You just need somewhere to rest your bum other than on the toilet seat, which can break off its hinges if used too much as a chair.

# Bathroom windows

It's a shame to lose a pretty view, but sometimes privacy has to take priority. This is obviously true in bathrooms, but there are ways to preserve modesty that are a positive asset.

One of the items I'm most fond of at Meadowgate is the bathroom blind, which is made out of a white linen breakfast cloth that has the prettiest embroidery and cutwork. Whenever I'm out and about in antiques warehouses I'm always foraging in baskets of old linens and coming across beautiful old tablecloths, but the words 'breakfast cloth' always made my heart sink because I thought I had no practical use for these small squares. But since having the blind made, I snap up these breakfast cloths. They're perfect for any room with one window, and it's lovely to find a practical use for an item that modern life doesn't really call for. (See page 106 if you fancy making a blind yourself.)

# Mirrors and glass

If you're limited for space in your bathroom, consider covering an entire wall in mirror glass. It's a bit of a pain to clean, but absolutely worth it. Mirror does wonders for creating the illusion of size in any small space, and mirror glass is actually quite cheap to buy.

Apart from their space-creating properties, mirrors are also fantastic at reflecting light and making rooms seem brighter. Who made the rule that there should be only one mirror in a room and that it should always be over the sink or a fireplace? I think it's a great idea to have several mirrors in a room, all of them bouncing light off each other or reflecting pretty exterior views. You can pick them up very cheaply in charity shops or antiques warehouses, often in quite eccentric frames, and you can paint or gild or distress them to match your scheme.

In the children's bathroom I wanted to try something a bit different, so, having opted for a seaside-inspired theme, I decided to make a leaded light-catcher, with the help of Amanda Winfield, a talented artisan who's been creating stained-glass pieces for the last 20 years.

The one thing I'll say about working with stained glass is that it's not one for the 'all-thumbs' klutzes among us, and I had a few crashes, smashes and scares when I was scoring and cutting out the pieces. But the process one goes through to make a leaded light is fascinating, and it's something that has changed little since medieval times.

I drew out my shapes on a piece of paper and, with Amanda's guiding hand, managed to cut the shapes from different coloured glass. Then

I put the pieces together, soldering them with lead. It was lots of fun, and I'd definitely recommend you try a one-day course and create your own one-off piece (see pages 186 and 218 for more details).

## Accessories and candles

There's been an ad on telly recently for battery-powered scented candles. The idea is that you get the glow and the scent, but without the real flame. Surely that's like baking a cake and not licking the bowl? Even if you think your chances of lighting candles and spending more than two minutes in the bath are going to come around less often than Christmas Day, they're still a lovely decoration, and candle-making is definitely in my top three rainy day activities (see page 142). My children are fascinated by the process of watching the wax melt in a pan, and I get the prize of the candle. It's a win-win craft, and for me, candles are lovely in a bathroom.

If you can't fill your bathroom with beautiful shelves and glass jars and candles, at least try to create a small corner for yourself – and if you have a family bathroom, do bear safety aspects in mind. In my bathroom in Devon sits a crystal urn that is badly broken on one side and stuck back together, but it's where I keep all the lotions and potions for my face and it's a no-go area for the kids.

I love having a real mishmash of bits in the bathroom. Toothbrushes and toothpaste in our house sit in giant royal jubilee mugs. One bathroom has a high shelf for the children's christening presents, which they love to look at and point out when they're in the bath. My other half has an extraordinary collection of odds and sods, including a silver cup won by his grandfather and a load of framed birthday pictures that the children have done for him.

I think there are lots of things people are afraid to put in bathrooms because steam might ruin them, but regulations on ventilation for bathrooms are so stringent these days that high condensation levels are rare. And if you do have a bathroom that's prone to condensation, you'll know about it way before you've had a chance to hang anything on the walls. I have pictures, photographs, ornaments and drawings from my children in the bathroom and they've come to no harm.

# Express yourself

The great thing about bathrooms, and small rooms in general, is that they're a fantastic way of indulging or displaying any passions, eccentricities or collections – I have a real passion for wallpaper and decided to cover my downstairs loo in a paper I made with the printmaker Emma Molony (see page 150). The design is powerful, yet it really works in a small room. I absolutely love that space.

Displaying old glass bottles or jars on a bathroom windowsill or shelf can look really pretty. These sorts of individual pieces can be picked up on the Internet and at reclamation yards or antiques shops everywhere. You could start your glass collection today.

In small spaces like bathrooms little details really stand out, meaning you can give your favourite ornamental pieces a home where they can take centre stage and look great. My friend Sasha has all sorts of weird and wonderful things in her bathroom, including a driftwood model boat and a slab of stone with fossilised fish on it. They both look just right in that context, as does the loo brush that sits in an old terracotta flowerpot on a matching drip-tray in her 'smallest room' near the garden. (Note that terracotta is porous, which is fine on a stone floor, but not on wood or carpet, as these will eventually rot.)

# Reading matter

You'll have heard me say this before, but wherever there's a loo, there must be reading matter. I favour *Vanity Fair* and a host of interiors magazines, while my other half has a huge pile of out-of-date Sunday supplements and *Country Life*. When I visited Hilary Charlesworth, the spinner and weaver featured on page 185, I was unbelievably impressed to find a collection of specs – yes, I do mean glasses – in her downstairs loo so that people can peruse the extraordinarily varied pile of reading matter when they use her bathroom. I'm definitely stealing that idea.

# Children's corner

A room specifically reserved for children to play in is a huge luxury that most people don't enjoy, so there are two ways of approaching a playroom. If you cannot sacrifice an entire room for play, the second, more realistic, option is to set aside a corner of a dining room, sitting room or kitchen to cater for your kids and their mass of toys that can return to being an adult space after they've gone to bed.

However much I believe in second-hand being best, I can't constntly inflict this on my children. There will always be some very bright, very plastic toys they will want, and your pre-baby aesthetics will have to fall by the wayside – all the more reason, then, to try to find an aesthetically pleasing way of tidying up their mess with speed and ease.

## Storage ideas

Having good storage for children's toys will go a long way towards saving your sanity. My other half believes that the simplest solution is to pick up a selection of old trunks and suitcases and simply chuck the children's toys into them, but I live in fear of having to extract crushed little fingers from a heavy lid or a rusty hinge. That said, my three-year-old has a trunk full of toys underneath his cabin bed and, so far, he still has all ten fingers. Touch wood.

For the first few years, children will always want to play around your feet. Wherever you are, they are. And that is often in the kitchen, and thus where their toys will accumulate. If you're having a new kitchen put in and you have children under five, or plan on having kids in the not-so-distant future, then bow to the inevitable and simply include extra pan drawers so you can incorporate a certain number of those plastic toys in them.

It's also worth buying or making a number of fabric toy bags as these work really well, and they're easy for even the smallest person to get things in and out of. But as they grow, and toys change, these bags become less suitable. So, you ask yourself, where the heck am I going to store all those little Lego pieces? In your heart, you know that clear plastic boxes marked Lego, Transformers, trains and train track are the answer, so my advice is to buy the best, cheapest and most suitable boxes you can find and get freestanding (if possible) shelves put up to hold those boxes. (Unlike fixed shelves, these don't cause any damage to the walls and can be sold when you no longer need them.)

I still regret not going for a stack of freestanding hospital catering shelves I once saw. Although as ugly as sin, they'd have been easy to disguise with a light curtain hanging from a rod fixed around the outside. In fact, I'd disguise any toy shelves in the kitchen, freestanding or otherwise. My ideal would be to curtain them so that they look like an additional window.

Of course, you could have cupboard storage if you prefer, but if you do, make sure the doors fold right open and, if possible, go back flat against the sides. Swinging cupboard doors are just asking for little fingers to get mashed in them.

## Let the kids decorate

I'm a great believer in allowing children to do their own decoration. My kids are constantly painting, drawing and making things at our kitchen table, and of course they want to hang them up and share their treasures with their parents. That's why I love pinboards. They work just as well as fridge magnets and they're easy to make yourself. All you need is a piece of soft wood that can take pins (or a cheap pinboard), cover it with a piece of fabric, and your little darlings can display their artwork and make you proud. See page 129 for full instructions.

Kids love to collect things too, especially stickers, so let them have a dedicated space for their display. The back of the bedroom door is probably best – the paintwork won't be damaged by the adhesive, and, as an added bonus, it won't be the first thing you or visitors see when looking into the room.

# Children's bedrooms

Frankly, I don't like having plastic toys in my children's bedrooms. I prefer their bedrooms to be places of calm, housing slightly more educational stuff, such as books, pictures, wall maps and their soft toys. However, it needs constant policing to keep the plastic out, so my ideal is rarely realised.

At the risk of stating the obvious, children tend to play on the floor, so you need to maximise the floor space, which is often limited in a bedroom. Bunk beds are great, but even better are raised beds – and I don't mean the type in which you grow flowers (although there are some parallels between children and flowers, but that's another matter). If you want to know how much flower, I mean floor, space you have in your children's room, lie down and look up at the ceiling: you'll see the blank canvas more clearly.

Cabin beds are a piece of design genius and will allow you to have the floor space you need. They're basically bunk beds without the lower bunk, so you can use the space below for a cot if you've got two children sharing a room, or for storing toys and books, or for a little desk to sit at. My other half recently found a cabin bed at the side of the road with a sticker pricing it at £20. When he went in to give the £20 to the builders, they told him there was a second cabin bed he could also take if he wanted. Of course he took it. Now admittedly the bed bits are a slightly unorthodox size, so the mattresses I've had to purchase are a little more expensive than normal, but other than that, these beds are definitely the bargain of my year. I've never found a decent cabin bed for under £300, so two for 20 quid... (By the way, if you're trying to find a mattress for an old cot, crib, Moses basket, or any odd-sized children's bed, Natural Mat is a brilliant, helpful, speedy and efficient company, see page 214.)

My dream, which I am about to realise in my children's bedrooms, is the built-in cabin bed. I am a complete sucker for bed alcoves – any kind of bed alcove. In a large family where siblings share rooms, it's difficult for them to guard their own space, so having a little corner where they can draw the curtains and take some time to themselves is a really lovely idea. And they can do that with built-in beds. Having stuff built in does cost more, particularly in the case of bedroom furniture, where you can buy good-quality freestanding cupboards and drawers for around £250 at auction. But when you look at the price of a bunk bed, or even the price of your sanity when you don't have enough space for all their stuff, is having a bed built in such an overspend? That's definitely one for you to decide. Built-in cabin beds are my dream, but not everyone else's.

**Tip**
If you wallpaper a child's room, make sure the cot is not right up against the wall. Those wallpaper joins are very tempting to little fingers...

# Children grow...

The simple rule is: don't spend money on things children grow out of within a year.

One of the few new things I ever bought for the children was a changing table that adapts into a desk and bookshelf when they get older. This idea, that the furniture grows with the child, is incredibly important to me. It's so tempting when you're pregnant to stick up the Peter Rabbit frieze, buy the changing table, the cot and all the matching stuff, but it costs the best part of £1000 and lasts for only a year! For me, it's a complete anathema. If you want to have all that stuff, please consider buying it second-hand. Go on eBay now and type in 'nursery furniture' – you'll save yourself a fortune.

Of course, children grow up and their tastes change, but one thing they never grow out of is having their own space. At different ages a curtain around the bed provides a hiding place to play with favourite toys, write a secret diary or cuddle a girlfriend, causing slightly less embarrassment when Mum walks in! The rooms that I've decorated for the children in London all include a little curtain to give them a hiding space in bed that will see them through the years, unless their favourite colour changes.

Typically, my ten-year-old stepson declared that black was his favourite colour, so we came to a compromise and decided that a black-and-white check would be just as cool. I'll be using green-and-white stripes in one room, and I'm going to resist the temptation to go down the 'cow, pig, duck' route as someone who's currently three will be six agonisingly fast and I will have to replace the cows, pigs and ducks because they're for babies.

Again, as with a playroom or children's corner, any child's room must have a pinboard or reserved wall space, and a shelf for their treasures that they can reach, but that is out of reach of younger siblings until they are old enough to know not to touch. Always provide a place for drawings, postcards from granny, pupil-of-the-week badges, swimming awards, gymnastics certificates, drawings done in class, report cards... And then build shelves for storage. Children collect things, they start early and they go on for a long time.

I'm not going to bang on about how you shouldn't have computers or televisions in a child's room, but I will say that all sorts of trouble is caused by children using the Internet out of sight of their parents. And if adults shouldn't have TVs in their rooms, then children *definitely* shouldn't.

But beanbags – now there's a great little invention. They're a handy form of soft, easily moveable seating to have on your children's bedroom floor and they're great space savors too.

## Special something

The quilt that Jo Colwill made for my son has pride of place in his room. All its fabrics and pictures tell a story, and I know it's something he will treasure forever, but it did take a long time to make. If you want to undertake something slightly more manageable for one of your children, such as making a quilted cushion cover (see page 167), or the draught excluder I knitted with Suzie Johnson (see page 174), it's well worth it, even though you might feel that when they're little you don't have enough time to breathe, never mind quilt or knit, and that you'll be lucky to have it finished in time for them to take to university. There is no better feeling than giving something you've made to your child that can grow old with them.

# Garden and entertaining

I believe that gardens are an extension of the house – an additional entertaining space that needs just as much colour, planning and care as any of the rooms inside.

Whether it's a play area for the children or an outside dining room full of foliage and twinkly lights, when it comes to designing and decorating your garden remember to think about how you want that space to work for you. What would you like to see every time you look out your window? Where will you sit on a warm summer's day to read a book? Where are the sunniest spots for the plants that need lots of light and warmth to grow? Where can the kids kick a ball without ruining those lovely flowers?

After 40 years of neglect, the garden at Meadowgate needed lots of attention. It was an overgrown, boggy, clay mess when we arrived, so I really had my work cut out. The only problem was, I've always been a bit nervous in the garden. The words, 'Those aren't *weeds*!' always come flooding back to me from my childhood – my dad is a very keen gardener – so I decided to enlist the help of my great friend Clemmie Hambro, who had just completed a horticultural course and was longing for a project (despite being eight months' pregnant). I also visited other people's gardens to see what kind of ideas I could pinch for my own.

Bearing in mind that Meadowgate is (a) just half a mile from the sea, (b) a total clay pit, and (c) a holiday home, so unlikely to get much TLC, it had to be the school shoes of the garden world – serviceable and low maintenance. Thankfully, it's not a huge garden: it goes around the house rather than leaning heavily to any one side, so I used this to my advantage, giving different parts of the garden different jobs to do.

Being so close to the sea, I wanted to introduce a maritime theme, so I painted the house in lovely blue and white and put an old rowing boat outside. I wanted a patio that I could use as both a sitting and eating area, but it had to be separate from the children's play area that Clemmie created in a little woodland by the back door. More than anything I wanted lots of vibrancy and colour that would last through the seasons. I managed this by adding furniture and planting flowers that would come out at different times of the year. I also made a delicious-smelling herb garden.

If you ask me, the garden at Meadowgate is blooming lovely. But, like all gardens, it's an everlasting project and still has a lot of growing up to do.

## Designing your outside space

Design statements can be just as powerful in our gardens as they are in our homes, and those eccentricities we bring out in the bathroom also have their place in the garden. One such garden I was lucky to visit while making *Homemade Home* belonged to mosaic artist Candace Bahouth. It's a space absolutely teeming with colour and vibrancy that really works all year round. As well as her incredible mosaic pieces – a mirrored egg, colourful obelisks and magnificent urns – Candace also hangs Perspex hearts, plants fake silk flowers and has bench-seating areas to make that space completely eye-catching. It may not be everyone's cup of tea, but honestly, what Candace does with her garden is brave, bold and, most importantly, it's completely personal to her.

**BELOW RIGHT:**
Some of the wonderful mosaic objects in Candace Bahouth's colourful garden.

Inspired by Candace, I wanted to inject some colour into Meadowgate's garden, so I made a small mosaic table to sit outside my back door . I love that little table (see page 154 to make your own).

# Smoke and mirrors

There are so many ways to make your garden shine. Mirrors dotted around give a fantastic illusion of space if your garden is on the *bijou* side, and extra colour and texture can be added with furniture. Old wire tables and chairs, vases, baskets, barrels and more can all do their bit. Even if they wither in the sun and rain, they develop a sort of patina that I think looks really pretty in a garden. So don't be afraid to use old indoor pieces that you no longer want inside in your garden.

Lighting is a real feature of a garden, but you don't need to go in for expensive electrical set-ups. Paper tea lanterns hung from trees in the summer look beautiful, and give out a gentle glow when the tealight inside them is lit as darkness falls. You can also use other types of lantern, like those Moroccan ones that have pretty patterns cut out of the metal, or just dot candles around (well out of children's reach). In the autumn or winter I love to build a fire outside to keep cosy; there's something very comforting about the flames lighting up the darkness.

There are lots of ways to illuminate your garden, but it can be an expensive business, so weigh up the costs and how much time you're really going to spend out there in the dark.

# Flowers

I love flowers, whatever the context. Garden displays and indoor arrangements both have a place in my heart, but I'm learning that what you grow in your garden or find growing wild can feed an otherwise expensive habit of buying from shops. Provided you plant a generous number of early risers, such as snowdrops, daffodils and tulips, you can nick a few for the house during the drearier months and enjoy their colour and scent throughout the home. Remember too that lavender, pansies and primulas are just as beautiful indoors as they are in your pots outside.

Later in the year flowers such as roses, hydrangeas, dahlias and gerberas allow you to 'cut and come again' for months on end. The thing about garden flowers is that you have to think ahead and get your bulbs or bedding planted in good time, but that planning is a lovely chore during the colder days of autumn and winter. Country house gardens and your local nursery are good places to visit if you want to be inspired on what to grow in your own garden and how to get that sunny lunch feel indoors and outdoors every day.

Lovely as cultivated blooms are, I think all flowers are up for grabs, and I have no rules about what I bring into the house. Some of the prettiest arrangements are made from wild flowers, such as pink willowherb, which grows along every hedgerow. Mix it with a few frothy stems of cow parsley and you have a pleasing display that's absolutely free.

When I decorate a table I always want to have flowers on it, but I like to keep arrangements simple and low, dotting them about at intervals, so they don't get in the way of eye contact or conversation. To me, paper whites in jam jars or a single rose that's been cut short and put in an eggcup are just lovely, and it can really make the difference to a table and your guests when they come over for tea or supper.

I learnt some fabulous ways with flower arranging from floristry expert Judith Blacklock, including my favourite tip of all time – the sticky-tape grid. If you don't know what that is, I urge you to turn right now to page 112.

# Home-grown

I've gone on a lot about buying things that are British and handmade, but I'm also a tremendous advocate of things that are home grown. At our house in Devon we keep a couple of chickens, grow a bit of our own fruit and veg, and also have a little herb garden that I use in my cooking all the time. During the summer, when the herb garden is in full bloom, the smells and colours are absolutely fantastic, but even in winter, you can still grow your own herbs indoors. It is easy to do, even if (like me) you're not naturally green-fingered. Clemmie inspired me no end, showing how simple it can be to make a little herb garden using an old tin bath I picked up for a tenner at a reclamation yard and a load of little herb plants that cost around £1.50 a pot. The entire thing was made for around £30. (See page 136 for a step-by-step guide.)

Since the house at Meadowgate is now restored, the garden tends to get most of my attention these days. Although I regularly add new pictures, pieces of furniture and other bits and bobs to the house, the garden is where I end up fiddling and fiddling and fiddling. It's effectively a new garden and Clemmie created a fantastic base, but I will have to carry it on and build on that base. It's a whole new experience for me.

# Eating outside

I love eating outside. And rain, hail, wind or shine, it *is* possible. The trick is to be prepared – and don't let the English summer, or a blustery cold day for that matter, get the better of you. A good tip is to invest in some small, cheap shoulder blankets that you can throw over the backs of chairs for guests to use when the night air creeps in.

One January, for my other half's birthday, I organised a winter picnic, and we dragged glass, silver, tablecloths, napkins, table decorations, proper plates – everything you can think to have on a table, we had it – up to an old shelter on top of a hill where you can see over Dartmoor and Exmoor. (By the way, when entertaining, even when it's an outside bash, I believe in dressing your table up to the nines. Paper plates are boring and unattractive, unless you've got a great big crowd or a kids' party, in which case they can work a treat). With the help of my sister, brother and his girlfriend, I laid the table with little Indian soldiers and elephants and silver beakers. This was a party for 20 people in the middle of January! Thankfully, the shelter has a rustically built barbecue, which we stoked up for warmth and all our guests were warned that this was a winter picnic. So as well as advising everyone to wrap up, I took lots of blankets and cushions to keep bums warm on the seats. The menu was beef bourguignon, baked potatoes and creamed leeks (pre-cooked and transported in a cool box with newspaper to insulate it).

We braved the outside elements for that occasion, but on days when you want that sunny lunch feel without the blustering wind, it is possible to bring the outside into your home by using fresh flowers, leaves, twigs and natural things that you can collect from the garden or outside.

**PREVIOUS SPREAD:**
A fantastic grass sofa created by Eloise Schwerdt and Helen Knight. Draped with a throw and scattered with cushions, it's the perfect place to relax outside.

# Entertaining

I am not very confident about my cooking. There are certain things I can do well, but let's just say I'm not a natural in the kitchen. So for me, a key part of feeding friends is getting the presentation right. If a table is set beautifully, it can make a huge difference to people's perception of the meal. Just as I've always been able to assess a property and see how to make the space work better, so I can look at china and glassware and see how to set it prettily.

I like to have as much food as I can on the table, rather than in the oven or elsewhere, because I think it makes for a more relaxed dinner. People sit down and just pass dishes around, and this also works really well if you're having take-away. You know the scenario – work overruns, you haven't had enough time to cook, the kids have been running riot and your guests are due to arrive in less than an hour. Order the take-away and set the table with tablecloth, napkins, cutlery, a few nice glasses and jugs of water. When the food arrives, put it in pretty bowls

and pop it on the table. *Voilà!* It's just about making the effort, and if you're not a great cook, this is the way to do it.

So often I hear the expression 'So and so tries too hard' and it's not meant as a compliment. I've always thought that sentence is idiotic. How can making an effort in life be anything less than a good thing? If you've made an effort to get a babysitter and put on your glad rags to go out to dinner at your friend's house, then it's nice to know that your host is as pleased to have you as you are to be there.

> **Tip**
> If you put a rosemary sprig in a jug of cold tap water, it disguises that slight chlorine taste you sometimes get. It also looks pretty and shows you've made an effort.

# Table linen

I always lay the table, but I wasn't brought up to do so. When I was younger, we only laid the table for guests coming, but I have noticed recently that the table at my mum's house is laid a lot more often than I remember from when I was young. Could this be that a working mum with four kids didn't have the time to lay the table with all of us running around her feet?

It is a fatal mistake to leave setting the table to the last minute. If you don't have kids, or if you have the luxury of a dining room, it's a good idea to lay the table the night before. Alternatively, gather together all the bits you would like on your table and put them in a box ready to go on the table the following day.

Start with a tablecloth. I have a number of tablecloths of which I am particularly fond. In fact, I nearly lost a friend over a lent and ruined tablecloth very recently – it was my favourite cloth and the one I used at the Meadowgate welcome lunch, so tears were shed! I always buy patterned or floral tablecloths because spillage marks show less. It's unavoidable that at some point someone will spill something, and when it happens, they feel bad, you feel bad, and neither of you can help but stare at it. Do you know why restaurants always have those crisp white cloths on the tables? It's nothing to do with aesthetics – it's because they're cheap and can be boil-washed.

I buy my tablecloths second-hand, but I have bought them new too. I set budgetary limits with all things I buy, but with tablecloths my spend is much higher than normal as I see them as an investment. Buy the right one and it lasts.

I'm now going to admit something, so prepare yourself for a shock... One of my favourite tablecloths is from...IKEA. I bought it many, many years ago, before I realised that such places were a false economy. But I love this tablecloth – it's blue and white and washes like a dream, and just shaking it over the table makes me feel more settled and organised about a dinner party.

I always put out napkins – not paper ones, but proper linen napkins. And I like to use napkin rings on really special occasions. I tend to buy my napkins in sets of six, but there's many a time when I have more than six people to dinner, so I use sometimes two, perhaps three, sets of napkin types on the table. Again, it's fine to mix and match. (See page 134 for how to fold napkins.)

# Tableware and glasses

I once had lunch with the late Mark Birley, the famous restaurateur and founder of Annabel's nightclub. On that table at lunch, every plate was different, every napkin was different, the cutlery wasn't all of a set. What *was* on the table was simply the prettiest stuff that he had found. We've been dominated by the matching mantra for far too long and for me it doesn't stick.

I like to serve food from some of my big bowls or serving plates, none of which match, but all of which just work together. Once you've embraced the idea of mixing and matching, you'll discover that it's an economical option too. And if you have the odd breakage, don't panic. The trick to mixing and matching your tableware is to have an order to it. I keep a sort of mathematical order to mine – if I have 12 people to dinner and I'm using a mixture of three sets of things – plates, glasses, napkins – I use four from each set and spread them evenly across the table. It's an eclectic, rather than chaotic, mix of things.

Something I absolutely adore is handmade glassware. It's a truly beautiful thing; you have to admit that it beats the mass-produced stuff hands down, and blown glass that you can buy from talented artisans all over the UK (see page 211) is something you'll always treasure. But, like most people, there was no way I could afford to kit out Meadowgate entirely with handmade glass, so I decided to buy just a couple of lovely tumblers to mix in with my cheaper stuff. Being thrifty isn't just about spending less; it's about spending wisely, and the few glasses I bought really make my kitchen table look great.

Keep your eyes peeled in charity shops and antiques warehouses and you can pick up mismatched items of pretty china and glass for a song. You can then have fun experimenting with the best way to use them. And remember, decorating a table is such an easy way to make your guests feel loved.

# When cooking for a crowd

I don't write place cards if I can help it as I have chronically bad handwriting – I mean completely illegible. But I always do a 'placement', scribbling down everyone's name on a piece of paper and shoving it in my pocket. Obviously, if you have lots of people coming to dinner, it is best practice to set down place names, and even for a small gathering, it's a lovely touch.

A good idea is to let your kids do the name tags – if you can persuade them – because (a) they'll look really sweet, and (b) it'll keep the little tykes busy while you get on with the rest of the table setting. There are lots of easy and fun ways to do place names – on bits of card or paper in brightly coloured felt-tips, on little pebbles with Tippex or nail varnish. You can even rope in some of the kids' toys, getting the children to fix name tags onto toy cars and little dolls.

At Christmas time I was shown how to do gold leaf pears as place settings. This was incredibly extravagant, and although I've no intention on splashing out on any more gold leaf for a dinner party, the pears were a great idea. Little luggage tags work a treat to pop onto the stem of each pear (or apple).

**PREVIOUS SPREAD:**
Who wouldn't feel celebratory at the sight of Sasha's table set so beautifully for a party?

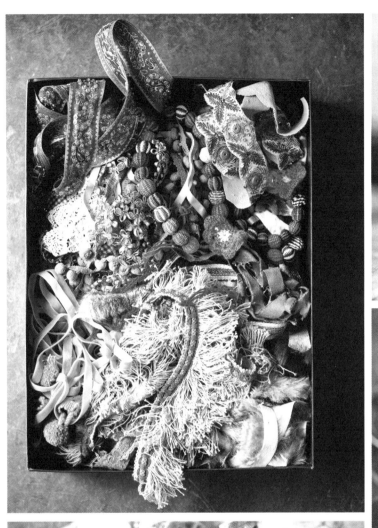

# Getting stuck in

# All sewn up

Textiles embody recycling in the home because they are the perfect way to change the look and feel of a room cheaply and easily. We live in a throw-away society, but my motto is 'Never throw anything away'. And that certainly applies to fabrics. I've got a huge basket of old linens, tablecloths, curtains and odd remnants of material – even the tiniest scraps can be useful when sewing, which is really the starting point to a whole host of projects I've included in this book.

Sewing is the ultimate in 'make do and mend', and there's no better way to make savings than by learning how to stitch. But it's not all about saving money. Taking the time to sew something can be an expression of love and care, and can also be a refuge from the crazy world. Trust me, focusing entirely on a needle, thread and cloth beats therapy any day.

Until recently, my ability pretty much stopped at sewing name tags onto the children's school clothes. But I was determined to add something to the soft furnishings pile at Meadowgate, and my mum's friend Chrissie Fearnehough, an interior decorator, agreed to give me a refresher course on the sewing machine and help me make a cushion.

With Chrissie's help, I discovered just how much you can do with a sewing machine. What's brilliant is that once you've got the confidence, you see everything for the opportunities it presents to you. So let your creative juices flow... And if you've never had a go on a sewing machine, or if this is your first time in years, believe me that putting your foot down on this pedal is just as big a rush as putting your foot down in a really fast car.

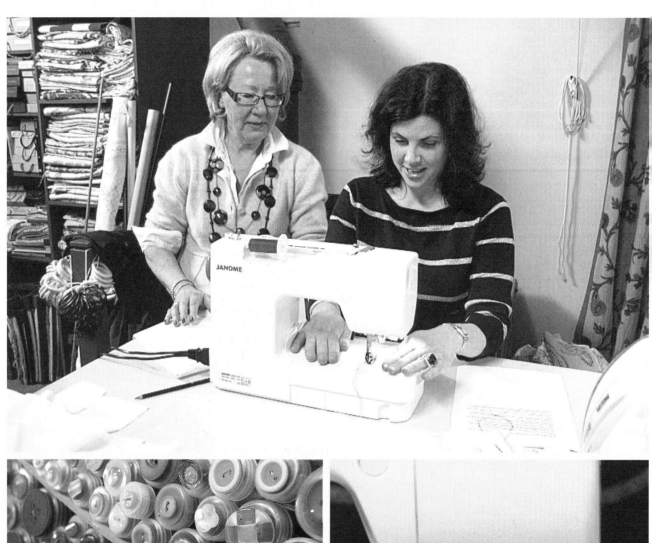

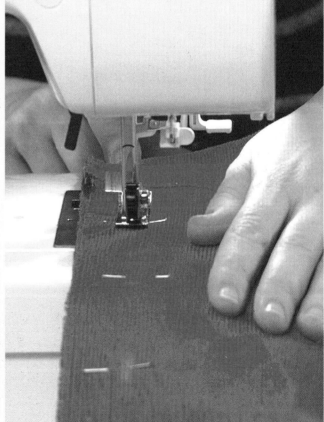

Sewing machines have come a long way since the days of treadles and hand-turned wheels. Nowadays, they're electronic and computerised, with all sorts of bells and whistles. They also vary widely in price, depending on how sophisticated they are. How on earth do you choose? Here are some points to bear in mind:

**1 How much sewing do you do?** If you're an occasional user, you'll probably need a fairly basic machine rather than one that does hundreds of different stitches. Keep it simple, and you're more likely to use it.

**2 What stitches will you need?** This depends on what you plan to make, but the vast majority of stuff can be made with straight stitch and zigzag. Buttonhole stitch tends to come as standard, while quilting stitch, overlocking, blind hem stitch and decorative stitches are found on more sophisticated machines. On the swankiest you can get more than 300 different stitches, but only professionals are likely to need those.

**3 What extras are worth having?** A basic machine comes with several presser feet, usually for straight stitch, zigzag, sewing narrow hems, stitching buttonholes and fitting zips. If you find you need others, you can buy them separately as the need arises. Another useful item is a free arm, which allows you to stitch in tight spaces, such as around cuffs and trouser legs.

**4 How much should you spend?** Sewing machines can cost anything from £50 to several thousand pounds. If you're making mainly household furnishings and fairly simple clothes, a basic model costing up to £100 will suffice. If you're planning to work with heavy upholstery fabrics, make tailored garments or do a lot of fancy embroidery, a sturdy mid-range model from £300 to £500 will probably meet all your needs.

**5 Where can you get expert advice before buying?** You can look online at various manufacturers' websites, such as www.singerco.com and www.berninasewingshop. co.uk. Even better, go into a store such as John Lewis (which also offers sewing classes), or your local sewing machine shop.

# LAVENDER BAG

These pretty little scented bags (made by Elanor Holland) are so easy to sew, and they make great presents (if you can bear to give them away). They are very speedy to run up on a sewing machine, but you could just as easily stitch them by hand. If you are lucky enough to grow lavender in your own garden, it's very easy to dry – simply pick a large bunch, tie the stems together with string, and hang it up somewhere out of the sun to dry. You can then strip all the flowerheads from the stems and enjoy the fragrance all over again.

**You will need**
- Remnants of pretty fabrics
- Tape measure
- Scissors
- Pins and needle
- Matching thread
- Sewing machine (optional)
- Ribbons and buttons
- Lavender, dried and stripped off the stem

**1** Cut out a piece of fabric measuring 18 x 15 cm (7 x 6 inches), using the fabric's selvedge (finished edge) as one the long sides. (If your fabric remnant does not have a selvedge, turn the raw edge over twice and stitch a narrow hem instead.) This will be the opening of the bag.

**2** To add a decorative ribbon band across the bag, cut an 18-cm (7-inch) length of ribbon, pin to the fabric and then stitch in place.

**3** With right sides together, fold the fabric in half widthways. Pin along the raw sides, taking a 1-cm (1/3-inch) seam, then stitch together.

**4** Trim the bottom corners on the diagonal, then turn the bag right side out.

**5** Cut another length of ribbon, fold in half to find the centre point, then hand-stitch this to the back of the bag about 3 cm (1¼ inches) from the top edge (this will be used to tie up the bag). Hand-stitch a button about 3 cm (1¼ inches) from the top on the front of the bag.

**6** To make the inner pouch for the lavender, cut another piece of fabric, this time measuring 18 x 12 cm (7 x 5 inches). Fold it in half and stitch up 2 sides, again taking a 1-cm (1/3-inch) seam. Turn the bag right side out and fill with lavender. Hand-stitch along the top to enclose the lavender.

**7** Pop the lavender bag inside your decorative bag and tie the ribbon, wrapping it around the button.

# DOORSTOP

This doorstop, made by Elanor Holland, is rather like an oversized version of the lavender bags (see page 100). Made from a heavy-duty fabric and filled with sand, it makes a far prettier doorstop than a piece of wood wedged underneath. If you have a sewing machine, you can whizz this up in minutes, but it's also quite a relaxing project to hand-sew. Just make sure you do the stitches tight or you'll end up with a beach by your door.

**You will need**
- Piece of heavyweight fabric, such as thick linen
- Tape measure
- Scissors
- Piece of braid
- Pins and needle
- Matching thread
- Sewing machine (optional)
- Cord
- Safety pin
- Plastic bag
- Sand
- Sticky tape

**1** Cut out 2 pieces of fabric measuring 15 x 30 cm (6 x 12 inches). Cut a 15-cm (6-inch) length of braid and pin it to one piece of the fabric, placing it equidistantly between the top and bottom. Stitch in place along its top and bottom edges. This is now the front of your doorstop.

**2** Fold over 2 cm (³/₄ inch) at the top of both the front and back pieces, turning it to the wrong side of the fabric. Pin and press, then stitch in place, leaving the ends open. This forms the channel for the drawstring cord.

**3** Place the front and back pieces together, right sides facing (so the braid is facing inwards). Pin around the 2 sides and the bottom, taking a 1-cm (¹/₄-inch) seam.

**4** Stitch around these 3 sides, starting just below the channel at the top, down the side, across the bottom, and up the other side, again stopping just below the channel opening.

**5** Trim the bottom corners on the diagonal to reduce bulk, then turn right side out.

**6** Thread the cord through the channel. The easiest way to do this is to attach a safety pin to one end, then use this to feed the cord through the channel.

**7** Fill a strong plastic bag with sand and seal the top with sticky tape. Pop the sandbag inside the fabric cover. Pull up the drawstring cord and knot the ends together.

# ENVELOPE CUSHION COVER

If you want to make a cushion cover like the one I made with Chrissie, and which now sits on the window seat in the Meadowgate kitchen, just follow these simple steps. The beauty of this type of cover is that it is made from just one piece of fabric and doesn't need a zip.

**You will need**
- Fabric
- Tape measure
- Scissors
- Pins
- Sewing machine
- Matching thread
- Cushion pad
- Buttons (optional)

**1** First, measure out the fabric. You need a piece of fabric 2½ times the length of the cushion, by the actual width of the cushion, plus an extra 5 cm (2 inches) on all sides for hemming or turnings. Cut out the fabric.

**2** With the wrong side of the fabric facing you, turn over 2.5 cm (1 inch) at each end of it, then turn over again to enclose the raw edges. Pin these double hems in place and press flat, then machine using a straight running stitch.

**3** With the right side of the fabric facing you, place the cushion pad in the centre of it. Fold the hemmed ends of the fabric over the cushion – this creates your 'envelope'. Use pins to mark the overlap.

**4** Remove the pad and pin the unhemmed edges together, keeping the overlap in place.

**5** Machine stitch along the 2 edges, 2.5 cm (1 inch) from the outer edge. Remove the pins.

**6** Neaten the edges by trimming to 1.5 cm (½ inch), then machine the edges with a zigzag or overlock stitch to prevent fraying.

**7** Turn the cover right side out. Press and then insert your cushion pad. If you like, you can add a couple of buttons to the cushion, purely for decoration.

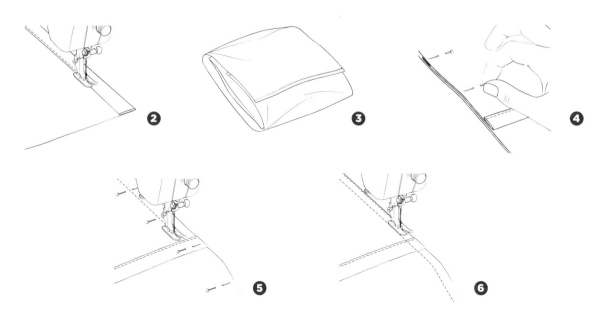

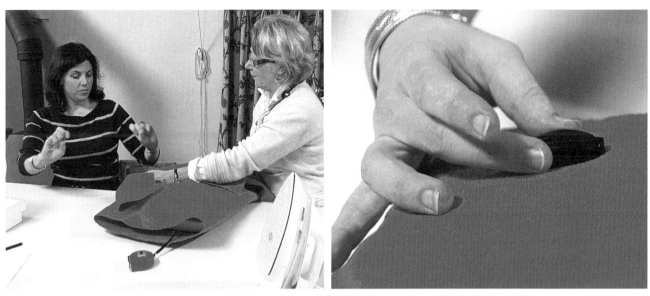

# LINEN BLIND

One of my favourite things at Meadowgate is the white linen blind that Chrissie and her team made for me out of an old breakfast tablecloth I found in my local antiques shop. I once saw a blind like this, many years ago, in the home of interior designer Anouska Hempel. It changed my view on the usage of old linen breakfast cloths forever.

Note: If you have no experience of sewing, making this blind could prove a bit challenging, so perhaps practise with some of the easier projects first. When you do decide to tackle it, a good tip is to make a sketch like the one below and put all your measurements on it as a handy reminder.

## You will need
- Tape measure
- Old linen tablecloth or other fabric
- Scissors
- Pins
- Matching thread
- Sewing machine
- Length of semicircular wooden batten, 3 cm (1¼ inches) in diameter
- Hacksaw (to cut dowelling and batten)
- Needle
- Small plastic roman blind rings
- Length of 5 x 2.5-cm (2 x 1-inch) wooden batten
- Staple gun
- Screw eyes
- Roman blind cord
- Cord weight
- Brackets
- Cleat

**1** Measure your window recess and decide whether your blind is to be fitted inside or outside the recess of window. Cut out the fabric as follows:

## WIDTH

**Inside recess:** Measure the width of the recess (A) and add 5 cm (2 inches) for hems (B).

**Outside recess:** Measure the chosen finished width of the blind (A) and add 5 cm (2 inches) for hems (B).

When cutting out the fabric, if it has a central design (as on my linen tablecloth), the centre of the design should be in the centre of the window.

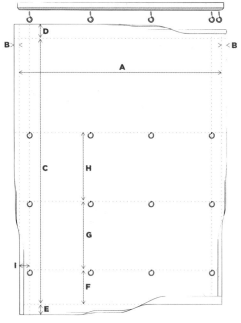

Dotted lines indicate folds and alignment.

## LENGTH

**Inside recess:** The finished length of the blind (C) is the drop of the recess (i.e. from top to bottom). Add 11 cm (4½ inches) to this measurement for hems – 6 cm (2½ inches) at the top (D) and 5 cm (2 inches) at the bottom (E).

**Outside recess:** The finished length of the blind (C) is the drop of the recess, plus 20 cm (8 inches). Add 11 cm (4½ inches) to this measurement for hems – 6 cm (2½ inches) at the top (D) and 5 cm (2 inches) at the bottom (E).

**2** With the wrong side facing you, fold over 2.5 cm (1 inch) of fabric down each side of the blind. Tuck the raw edge inside each fold, then pin, press and machine-stitch in place.

**3** Cut the semicircular batten to 2.5 cm (1 inch) less than the width of your blind. On the bottom edge of the blind you need to make a casing for it. Again with the wrong side facing you, fold over 5 cm (2 inches) of fabric, then turn the raw edge under by 1 cm (⅓ inch). Pin and machine-stitch along the edge. Do not insert the batten yet.

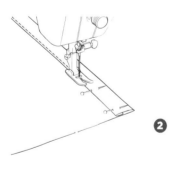

②

③

**4** Neaten the top edge of the blind by making a single hem. With the wrong side facing you, simply turn over 1 cm (⅓ inch) fabric, pin it and machine in place.

**5** Decide how much you wish your blind to hang down when folded up at the window and make a note of the figure. Doing maths was never my strong point, but now you need to make the following calculation:

Subtract 4 cm (1½ inches) from the finished length of the blind, then divide this figure by 3.5. For example, if the finished blind is 120 cm (47 inches):

$$120 - 4 = 116 \div 3.5 = 33.1 \text{ cm}$$
$$(\text{or } 47 - 1\tfrac{1}{2} = 45\tfrac{1}{2} \div 3.5 = 13 \text{ inches})$$

Now divide this figure by 2 = 16.6 cm (or 7½ inches)

Add the 4 cm (1½ inches) back on: 16.6 + 4 = 20.6 cm (or 7½ + 1½ = 9 inches)

This is the amount by which the blind will hang down when pleated up. If it doesn't match the drop you had in mind, you might have to divide by 2.5 or even 4.5 instead of 3.5. Alternatively, you might wish to adjust the position of the fold lines so that they don't obscure the central design on the fabric.

**6** With a line of pins, mark the following pleat lines across the back of the blind.

In our example:
1st line (F) is 16.6 cm (7½ inches) up from the bottom
2nd line (G) is 33.1 cm (13 inches) up from 1st line
3rd line (H) is 33.1 cm (13 inches) up from 2nd line

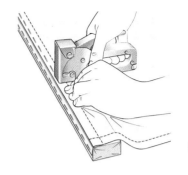

Stitch the plastic rings along these lines to carry the cords for the blind. Position the outermost rings 5 cm (2 inches) from each side (I), then evenly space those in between, leaving no more than 40 cm (16 inches) between rings.

**7** Cut the rectangular batten to the same width as your blind. Cover it with leftover fabric and staple in place along a 2.5-cm (1-inch) side. Staple the top of your blind along the top back edge of a 5-cm (2-inch) side.

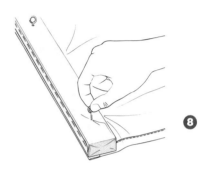

**8** On the underside of the batten (the 5-cm/2-inch side), screw in the screw eyes to line up with the rings you have sewn on. Position 1 extra screw eye 1 cm (⅓ inch) in from whichever side you wish to pull up the blind.

**9** Tie cords to the bottom rings on the fabric. Thread them up through each line of rings above, then through the screw eyes along the batten to the final screw eye at the pull-up side. Now thread all the cords into a cord weight and tie off.

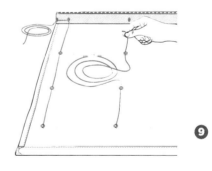

**10** Insert the semicircular batten in the channel at the bottom of the blind and hand-stitch the open ends closed.

**11** Fix the batten to the wall or window frame with small brackets. Screw a cleat to the side wall in a direct line below last screw eye.

# Beautiful things

## Flower arranging

I like to have flowers in the house *full stop*. It's the way the scent and colours bring a room to life. Flowers have been used to decorate homes for centuries and, as children, I'm sure you've all picked them from gardens as a present for a loved one. I'm forever pinching lavender from people's gardens, and in Devon we always have flowers in the house, even if it's only greenery and berries. When in London, I definitely have to be a bit more price-conscious, but the other day I did a deal with myself that for every month I didn't get any parking tickets, I would allow myself fresh flowers in the house.

When it comes to picking flowers, I simply tend to go with what I like and what I think might work together. Even if it's just some snowdrops in a jam jar, it makes such a difference to have them on a table. My favourite quick, clever trick is sticky tape over a shallow bowl, which I learnt from expert florist Judith Blacklock when she came to help me dress the rooms with flowers at Meadowgate. It was an absolutely brilliant idea, and helped turn a bunch of narcissi into a firmly anchored explosion of colour. Follow Judith's instructions for this, and for an easy-to-master hand-tied bouquet, in the following pages.

# STICKY-TAPE GRID

I'm sure that, like me, you'll be amazed at this simple yet effective technique from Judith Blacklock. Say goodbye to droopy stems and hello to a whole new world of stunning flower arrangements.

**You will need**
- Roll of sticky tape
- Shallow bowl
- Short stems of seasonal flowers (this idea is particularly effective for spring and bulb flowers, which like their ends to be in water rather than florists' foam)

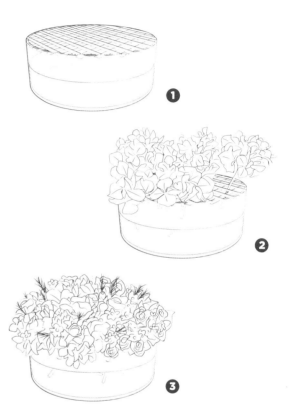

**1** Place strips of sticky tape at regular intervals across the top of the bowl, first in one direction, then in the other direction, at right angles. The spaces you make need to be of a size that give support and take the stems easily.

**2** Carefully pour fresh water into the container. Place the stems of your chosen flowers through the grid: the heads should rest on it. The photos show hydrangea, which gives bulk quickly and easily. Further stems, in this case narcissi, can be pushed through the hydrangea florets.

**3** Cut the stems of your other flowers and bits of greenery to a similar length and insert through the grid.

# HAND-TIED BOUQUET

Making a hand-tied bouquet can be a little tricky the first time you try it, but the technique is easy to master and soon you'll be able to create the perfect bunch of flowers with a spiral of stems that adds to the overall impact.

Avoid selecting flowers that branch down or have weak stems that will break easily on handling. As your hand-tied bouquet needs to have immediate impact, choose flowers with a strong form, such as gerberas, sunflowers, open roses or peonies.

**You will need**
- 25–35 stems of flowers and foliage
- Scissors
- Raffia or twine

**1** Remove the foliage and thorns from the bottom two-thirds of the stems, but always try to leave at least one leaf at the top.

**2** Decide what height you want the tied bunch to be and remove any obvious excess length from the end of the stems. This will make the bunch lighter to hold when assembling.

**3** To create a spiral of stems, hold the first stem vertically in your left hand (or your right if you are left-handed), using the thumb to keep it in position. Keep your fingers together. Cross a second stem over the first with the head of the flower towards the shoulder of the hand holding the flowers.

**4** Take further stems of flowers or foliage, one at a time, and repeat the previous step, always angling the head towards the shoulder of the hand holding the flowers.

**5** If you feel your design is unbalanced in colour, form or texture (this will happen a few times as you build up your bouquet), add a stem behind the arrangement by simply lifting the fingers. It should be angled in the opposite direction to all the other stems. This is the only other movement involved.

**6** Once all the stems have been added, hold the bunch very tightly and wrap with raffia or twine as high up the stems as possible, just below the lowest foliage. Cut the stems neatly to the same length.

# Cake decorating

Cake – just the word makes me smile, and like lots of you, I'm sure, I love to have a go at baking whenever there's a hint of a celebration, and even when there's not. Until recently, the most I'd ever done to decorate the top of my sponge was a slap of butter icing. Anything else seemed to need too much concentration, preparation and patience – and I'm not known for my patience.

But then I was introduced to Mich Turner. Anyone who meets Mich will sit up and pay attention – she decorates cakes beautifully, and I was entirely engrossed when she taught me a few tricks to turn mini cakes into masterpieces. Believe me when I say that it's just as much fun to decorate cakes as it is to eat them. Or maybe it's because you can eat them that I loved it so much. And to top off my day with Mich, I got to sprinkle my cakes with glitter – the type that it's ok to eat (in small quantities). Edible glitter – possibly the best combination of words in the English language.

But when did it all turn edible art? Cake decorating kicked off in the mid-seventeenth century, when Europe's aristocracy began to display elaborately decorated cakes at their banquets, though they were very rarely eaten. There's fat chance of a crumb being left on any plate in my house, but like those posh parties in the seventeenth century, cakes remain the most revered and welcome guests at the centre of our celebrations. They've gone way past that 'smartie tooth smile' and skooshy cream trim, made famous by Grandma and the WI (although I personally love a bit of skooshy cream). This is a great home craft and it's fantastic fun for friends and children alike.

The decorating ideas Mich showed me were candy-striping and how to make a handmade rose with iced leaves. I applied both of these to mini cakes, which are the ideal size for a beginner to work on. It means that if you make a mistake, it's a much smaller sin to eat it and start again!

If you've got the knack and you love to decorate cakes, you can take master classes at cake-decorating studios all over the UK, or you can get sugarcraft qualifications online and study from your own kitchen (see page 206).

After Mich taught me how to make my sugarpaste roses, I decided to have a go with playdough at home – it was a great way to practise, and I found myself making loads of little roses on the kitchen table. Then, of course, my son came over, and with one little paw he squished them...

# HANDMADE ROSE

**You will need**
- Sugar paste in the colour you want your rose
- Small sharp knife
- A4 plastic sleeve (the sort you get in stationery shops), slit so that 3 sides open like a book
- Edible glitter
- Mini sieve (or a tea strainer)
- Nozzle-less piping bag (or a sandwich bag)
- Green royal icing (again, you can buy or make your own)
- Plain iced mini cakes or a simple iced round cake (made or bought by you)
- Delicate, nimble fingers

**1** Start by making the petals. Tear off a small piece of your coloured sugar paste, knead well and roll into a sausage about 2.5 cm (1 inch) in diameter (the width of a 10p coin). Slice the sausage into 6 little circles each about 3 mm (⅛ inch) thick.

**2** Lay out the circles inside your plastic sleeve, fold the flap over them and squish them down once with the palm of your hand. Press each one lightly with your thumb to flatten the top part of the edge, then lift back the plastic.

**3** Now look for the smallest flat circle you've made and pick it up by the thick end (not the end you gave the additional press with your thumb). If you give it a gentle push (rub it from underneath with your thumb) and a peel, it should stay in one piece as it lifts off, and you end up with a nice curl to it.

**4** Hold the petal between your thumb and forefinger and gently, starting on one side, curl it over on itself to form the centre of your rose.

**5** Lift the next petal off the plastic in the same way as before. Turn it over and balance it on your finger. Place your central petal on it with the seam in the centre about halfway down. Squeeze the outer petal around it and pinch together at the base. Gently press the top edge of the outer petal downwards with your finger to curl it slightly.

**6** Do the same again with a third petal, but place it on the opposite side of the second petal. Keep going like this until you've secured all six petals. It should be looking like a beautiful rose now.

**7** Using a small sharp knife, gently slice off the bottom of the flower so it has a flat base and will sit level on top of your cake.

**8** Now it's glitter time! Spoon some glitter in a mini sieve and dust it over the top of the rose so it's all pretty and sparkly.

**9** To make the leaves, take your piping bag and fill it with the green icing. Twist the bag closed, then cut the pointed end of it into a little V-shape. Practise the next bit on a flat surface first to get the hang of it. You squeeze the bag and sort of wiggle it up and down to make a rippling leaf shape, pulling it away to leave a point at the end. When you're feeling confident, make 3 leaves on top of your cake. Sit the sparkly rose on top and *voilà* – a beautiful and delicious creation!

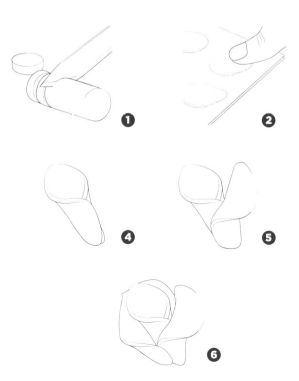

# CANDY-STRIPING

**You will need**
- 3 piping bags
- 3 x size 3 piping nozzles
- 3 different colours of royal icing
- Plain iced mini cakes or a simple iced round cake (made or bought by you)
- A very steady hand – don't do this one with a hangover

**1** Fit each of the 3 piping bags with a nozzle and put a different colour of icing in each one.

**2** Hold the piping bag, using both hands to balance it and keep it steady. (It's good idea to start off with white icing because if your hand is a bit wibbly, like mine was, the mistakes are much less noticeable.) Make contact with the top edge of the cake, squeezing the bag gently so the icing comes out. Draw the piping bag a little away from the cake as you pipe a stripe down the side and seal it at the bottom. ('Sealing' means that you hold the nozzle still for a moment until a 'pearl' forms, then lift the bag away.)

**3** Keep going like this, alternating the colours, all the way around the cake. It will take practice and probably a few cakes to get right, but who cares when your mistakes are still delicious?

# GILDING GLASS

Nowadays, when we think of gilding, what usually comes to mind are ornate gold frames around paintings and mirrors. But gilding can be done in silver as well as gold, and on many different surfaces.

Gilding on glass, also known as *verre églomisé*, is an extremely beautiful way of using gold and silver leaf. Under glass, silver becomes soft and reflects the light like an antique mirror, while gold shimmers richly. As gilding expert Christine McInnes told me, there are many different techniques, most of them extremely complex and time-consuming, but the one used here is simplified to get you started. Copying a design through the glass and backing it with silver is an easy way of achieving a very pretty result without needing to have a lot of artistic experience. Don't be frightened of working with silver leaf: it's actually much easier to work with than gold. Just be careful to keep your books of silver leaf away from water at all times, and if you find your hands trembling when you're laying it on the glass, support your elbows to give you more control.

**You will need**
- Piece of glass (usually 3–4 mm/⅛ inch thick, but not terribly important)
- Cotton cloth
- Image to copy
- Sellotape or Blu-Tack
- Artist's brushes (synthetic is fine): no. 5 for general use, no. 000 for fine detail, and a 1.5-cm (½-inch) brush for applying the gelatine wash
- Glass paints, water-based or oil-based, or artist pigments mixed in a solution of shellac (1 part pigment to 6 parts shellac)
- Small glass jars (to mix pigments with shellac)
- Methylated spirits (to wash brushes if using shellac)
- Gelatine capsules (2 mixed in a cup of hot water); at a pinch, use ½ teaspoon supermarket gelatine in a cup of hot water
- Talcum powder (optional)
- Loose silver leaf (*not* transfer leaf)
- Cotton wool
- Backing paint, such as black acrylic or emulsion (optional)
- Household paintbrush (optional)

Most of the materials needed for this project can be bought from an artists' supply shop. The silver leaf and capsule gelatine are available from gilding suppliers.

**1** First clean your piece of glass with a cotton cloth.

**2** Place the image you wish to copy on a flat surface. Position the glass over it and secure with either Sellotape or Blu-Tack.

**3** You now have to copy your image onto the glass using a technique called reverse painting, so look carefully and work out what should be painted first. If you are painting a flower, for example, paint the delicate details like the stamens first, and then the background petals. The reason for this is that you will be looking *through* the glass from the other side to see your final image. It's no use painting petals and then the stamens because the latter will only be visible on the back of the glass, not the front. Take a little time to think about this and it will become clear. Just remember that you are working on the *back* of the glass.

**4** Once your image has been painted onto the glass, allow it to dry (20 minutes for shellac colours, overnight for glass paints).

**5** Mix up the gelatine water. Dip the 1.5-cm (½-inch) brush fully in the mixture and liberally wet the glass on the painted side, brushing gently as the paint is delicate.

**6** Make sure your hands are completely dry and keep all water away from your book of silver leaf. If your hands are hot, you can use a little talcum powder on them to stop the silver sticking to you.

**7** Lift up a sheet of silver leaf and slowly lower it onto the wet glass – don't breathe too much! You'll find that it is sucked down by the water, so let that happen. Take another sheet of silver and repeat the process, making sure that it slightly overlaps the first sheet. Carry on until your piece of glass is completely covered in silver.

**8** Leave overnight to dry. If you want to speed up the process, use a hair-dryer.

**9** When the leaf has dried, take a small piece of cotton wool and gently rub all over the surface of the silver. This will remove any loose pieces and also burnish the surface. If there are any areas where silver is missing, reapply some gelatine water and patch them with small pieces of silver leaf. This shouldn't be necessary if the glass is thoroughly wet the first time around. (Gilders call the patching process 'faulting'.)

**10** If you wish to protect the silver leaf, apply a coat of backing paint and leave to dry. Gilders traditionally use black with silver, and it looks very beautiful, but you can use a different colour if you want.

# SOAP-MAKING

Making soaps is Jenny Elesmore's passion. She's been doing it for over ten years. Using traditional methods and only the finest ingredients, Jenny whisks each batch by hand and decorates them to create beautiful bars of soap that smell good enough to eat.

Try her method, using just a few household ingredients, to make your own. The quantities below make about 30 x 100-g (4-oz) bars of soap. You can add whatever fragrances and textures you like, but the suggestions below – parsley and lime; lemongrass, oats and honey; cinnamon and orange – are absolutely divine.

Note: Protective clothing and goggles are essential when making the soap because the fumes and heat given off by the caustic soda are pretty strong.

**You will need**
- Measuring jug
- Water (mineral or tap)
- Big plastic bucket
- Apron or protective clothing
- Safety goggles
- Rubber gloves
- Accurate kitchen scales
- Caustic soda (available from hardware shops and large supermarkets)
- Whisk
- Coconut oil (available from specialist shops and online; vegetable fat from the supermarket can be used instead)
- Large saucepan
- Kitchen thermometer
- Sunflower oil
- Good-quality olive oil
- 3 x 1-litre (2-pint) bowls (1 per fragrance); if making just 1 fragrance, a plastic bucket is fine
- Essential oils, e.g. lime, lemongrass, cinnamon
- Dried herbs, e.g. parsley
- Fine oats
- Runny honey
- Chopped orange peel
- 3 x 1-litre (2-pint) plastic moulds for shaping the soap (1 per fragrance; or use various small plastic containers, such as yogurt pots, or even ice-cube trays)
- Tray large enough to hold the moulds
- Blanket
- Greaseproof paper
- Thin slices of orange, for decoration (optional)
- Sharp kitchen knife or metal cookie cutters

**1** Measure 930 ml (33 fl oz) water and pour it into a bucket.

**2** Do this step outside if possible. Wearing protective clothing, goggles and rubber gloves, carefully add 295 g (11 oz) caustic soda to the water. (Caustic soda is a cleaning agent essential to the soap's six-week curing process, but it leaves no caustic properties in the final soap product, so is safe to include.) Stir the mixture with a whisk. The two ingredients will react together, producing heat and steam. Be careful not to inhale this. When it's finished reacting, set aside.

**3** Measure 615 g (22 oz) coconut oil into a large saucepan. Melt it over a medium heat, keeping a close eye on it as it melts fast. When it reaches 35–36°C (95–98°F), remove from the heat and add 800 ml (28 fl oz) sunflower oil and 800 ml (28 fl oz) olive oil.

**4** Pour the oils into the bucket of caustic soda and water. Stir regularly with a whisk for about 45 minutes, until there is a change of colour or texture in the mixture – you're looking for something called 'trace'. This is the point where the mixture has thickened and a drizzle of it leaves a line on the surface. Tracing can occur quickly or slowly, but on average takes 40 minutes.

**5** Divide the mixture equally between your 3 bowls.

**6** Measure 20 ml (4 teaspoons) lime essence into your first bowl. Add a handful of dried parsley and stir well.

**7** Measure 20 ml (4 teaspoons) lemongrass essence into your second bowl. Add a handful of oats and 2 tablespoons of honey. Mix well.

**8** Measure 20 ml (4 teaspoons) cinnamon essence into your third bowl. Add some chopped orange peel for texture and fragrance. Stir well.

**9** Lightly grease your moulds with sunflower or olive oil; this will later ease the removal of the finished soap. Place the moulds on a tray and pour in the soap mixture, leaving at least a 2.5-cm (1-inch) space at the top.

**10** Cover the moulds with a blanket and leave for 24 hours to set. If you want to add orange slices for decoration, do so while the soap is still slightly soft: simply place them along the top of the soap at regular intervals.

**11** When the soap is firm, turn it out, place on greaseproof paper and leave to dry in a cupboard or somewhere you won't touch them for 6 weeks. (It takes this long for the caustic soda to lose its caustic properties.)

**12** If you want to cut the soaps into bars, do this within 24–36 hours of setting or the blocks will be too hard. Wearing rubber gloves and using a sharp knife, simply cut the soaps into bars with a knife, place on greaseproof paper and leave to cure as described above. If you want to cut the soap into fancy shapes, you can use metal cookie cutters.

# STENCILLING PICTURES

Stencilling is fantastic! It's so easy to do, yet the results look amazingly professional. I was taught how to do it by Helen Morris, who runs The Stencil Library, a treasure trove of designs to suit all levels of ability.

A stencil is simply a cut-out that you paint over in multiple places to reproduce pattern on a surface. And that surface can be virtually anything – walls, floors, furniture, fabric... In the second TV series, Helen demonstrated how to make stencilled blinds, but here the technique is applied to a trio of canvases to create a striking wall decoration.

The canvases can be stencilled in their raw state, or a background colour of matt emulsion can be applied. In that case, it's a good idea to pick a shade found elsewhere in the room where the pictures will hang. Of course, the colours of the design itself can also reflect your colour scheme.

The design used here is a lovely arrangement of twigs and leaves, which have been laid out to 'escape' from one canvas to another. If you like, the design could escape even further and spread onto floors, furniture or fabrics, as shown opposite with a cushion cover. The point is that a stencil can be used over and over again in any number of ways and colours to get exactly the look you want. The only limits to what you do are time and imagination.

**You will need**
- 3 stretched canvases (the ones here measure 61 x 74 cm/24 x 30 inches)
- Matt emulsion (optional, but taupe is used here)
- Pencil and paper
- Stencil LTL 5 small from The Stencil Library (see page 219)
- 3 stencil brushes (1 large, and 2 small to medium brushes for outlining – you need 1 for each colour)
- Water-based paint (antique gold, raw umber and burgundy are used here)
- Palette or foil container (like those used for mini fruit pies)
- Kitchen roll
- Low-tack tape (*not* ordinary masking tape)
- Scissors

All the materials needed for this project can be bought from craft shops or post-free from stencil-library.com.

**1** Decide if you want a background colour on your canvases. The ones here have 3 coats of matt emulsion in taupe. Allow to dry thoroughly between each coat and before you start stencilling.

**2** Set out the canvases on a flat surface to explore the display options – side by side or one above the other or however you like.

**3** Draw a sketch on a piece of paper to work out the flow of pattern over the canvases. It's best to have a fairly sparse arrangement of twigs and get the density of the pattern from the leaves.

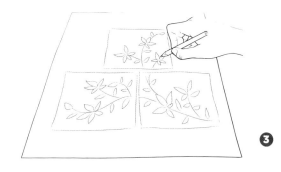

**4** The next step is to stencil some leaves onto paper to use later as templates. This will be done with the gold paint and the large brush, but please read the whole of this step before you start. Whenever possible, take the paint from the lid of the pot, otherwise put a shallow amount onto a palette or into a foil dish. Dip the tip of the large brush into the paint, then work it vigorously into a kitchen roll in a circular motion. This distributes the paint evenly over the bristles. Do a second circle on a clean patch of the roll to ensure that the bristle tips are damp rather than wet. To get the feel of how little paint should be used, tap the brush onto a corner of the paper and immediately run your finger over the mark. If it smudges, give the brush another circle on the kitchen roll. Now tape the stencil to your paper and apply the paint through the leaf-shaped holes, circling the brush (not dabbing) from one end to the other. The leaves should be dry within a second. Roughly cut around them and set aside for step 6.

**5** Now arrange a framework of twigs across all 3 canvases, keeping it pretty sparse. Tape the stencil in place. Dip the largest of the brushes into the gold paint, preparing it as described in step 4, and stencil the twigs. Carefully lift off the stencils.

**6** Before stencilling the leaves, work out where you'd like them to be by using the paper templates you made in step 4.

**7** Position the leaf stencil on the canvas, tape in place and start stencilling, again using the largest brush and the gold paint.

**8** To add depth to the design, you now outline random parts of some leaves with the burgundy and brown paint. Using a small to medium brush (1 for each colour), stencil close to the edge of the leaf shape. Your canvases are now finished and ready to hang.

**9** To clean the stencil, submerge it in hot soapy water, then place on a flat surface, such as a sink or bath, and gently work the paint from the holes using a stencil brush or your finger. Hang up or dry flat. Do not reuse until thoroughly dry. Also clean the brushes in hot soapy water, then rinse and leave to air-dry. They must not be used to stencil until thoroughly dry.

❹

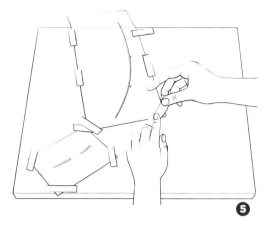

**⑤**

**⑥**

## CUTTING YOUR OWN STENCILS

If you would like to have a go at making your own stencil, you will need stencil film and a chinagraph pencil. Simply sketch the shape you want onto the film, then cut around it as described below. Complicated designs require ties or bridges to hold the shapes together, and it takes lots of experience to do this well so that the bridges are an integral part of the design. By all means have a go, but you might find it easier to take a class in the technique.

Once the design is drawn, it can be cut either with a craft scalpel or an electric heat pen. Place the film on a cutting mat (heat-proof if using a heat pen) and cut around your design. The pen is great for cutting intricate shapes, but you must relax and trace slowly to get clean edges. Once the shape has been cut, it can be lifted cleanly from the board.

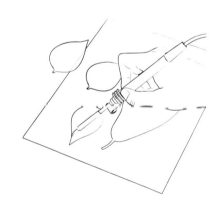

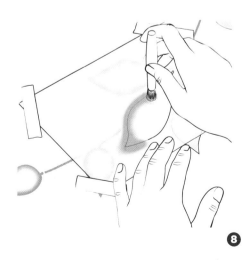

**⑧**

# Child's play

If the whole world of crafting is new to you, there's no easier way to dip a toe into those unknown waters than with the projects in this section. Over the next few pages are a few simple but very satisfying things to make, including a jolly-looking pinboard, some fun cosies made from old jumpers and a really useful herb garden. However, the craft I fell in love with, and highly recommend for its instant results, is découpage. Using remnants of fabric and any decorative bits and bobs you happen to have, you can transform boring or ugly objects into items worthy of display in a surprisingly short time.

     Believe me, anyone can turn their hand to the ideas that follow, and they really are perfect for doing with children. The kids can make lots of mess, which they adore, and still produce something that you and they will find useful and attractive. What more could you ask?

# PINBOARD

Pinboards are great for kitchens (for storing receipts, bills, 'to do' lists and all those annoying bits of paper that you can't throw away but can't find a home for either). They're also perfect for children's rooms, giving kids somewhere to create an ever-changing display of their own artwork, postcards and any other precious bits and pieces they collect. Elanor Holland devised this really quick and pretty way to turn an everyday pinboard into something special.

**You will need**
- Craft glue
- Cheap framed pinboard
- Piece of fabric, the same size as the pinboard
- Ribbon
- Scissors
- Drawing pins

**1** Spread a thin layer of glue all over the cork part of the pinboard, then cover with your choice of fabric. Using your palms and working outwards from the centre of the board, smooth the fabric out. Wipe away any excess glue around the frame.

**2** Cut strips of ribbon to run diagonally across the board in both directions, crossing at right angles. Push the ends of the ribbon under the frame and add a small dab of glue to hold in place.

**3** Push a drawing pin into the pinboard at each point where the ribbons cross over.

**4** If you wish, cut a further 4 lengths of ribbon to pin around the inside edge of the pinboard frame.

# SHRUNKEN JUMPER COSIES

It has happened to all of us. You're in a rush, you throw a load of laundry into the washing machine, and it's only when it reaches the end of its hot cycle that you realise your favourite hand-wash-only sweater is in there too, whirling around on a fast spin. But rather than shedding a few tears and consigning the now-unwearable felted jumper to the bin, try this clever idea from Penny Horne, and turn the ruined garment into these sweet cosies for your storage jars.

**You will need**
- Old woollies that have felted in the wash
- Scissors
- Storage jars or other items to be 'cosied'
- Felt-tip pen
- Pins
- Embroidery needle (a thick needle with a large eye)
- Embroidery thread

**1** Cut out the front and back panels of a jumper and lay them flat on a table.

**2** Lay the jar you want to 'cosy' flat on the jumper and draw around it, making sure the fabric will go slightly more than halfway round. Cut another piece to the same size. These will form the front and back pieces of your cosy.

**3** If you like, you can decorate the cosy at this point using contrasting colours of shrunken jumper or fabric. You could cut out a shape and embroider words on it, then stitch this to the front of the cosy. Or simply embroider words directly onto the cosy itself.

**4** Pin the front and back pieces together, right side out. If you wish to add a loop at the top, cut a small strip of fabric and fold in half. Insert at the top of the cosy and pin in place.

**5** Using embroidery thread in a contrasting colour, blanket-stitch up one side, over the top (securing the loop in place) and down the other side. Blanket-stitch over the raw edges of the bottom opening so they don't unravel, then pop the cosy over the jar you want to hide.

# FABRIC DECOUPAGE

Covering surfaces with offcuts of fabric is incredibly simple and great fun. It's easy enough to do with children, and a great way of transforming a plain or ugly object into something that's fun and individual, and that can add a decorative edge to your room. It's also a lovely idea for a gift if you're looking for something pretty, handmade and costing only pennies to produce.

It's best to start off with something small – a disposable tissue box, a fizzy drink bottle (Orangina has the perfect shape), or a ceramic teapot you've never been keen on (see the examples shown opposite, made by an artist in the craft, Penny Horne). Boot fairs and junk shops can be great sources of items that have interesting shapes. And once you're hooked, you could always graduate to items of furniture – a colourful table for the bedroom, a crazy lampshade, a blanket box or your very own customised chest of drawers.

If you don't have any suitable remnants lying around, you can buy offcuts for next to nothing from your local fabric shop, or try Indian markets for wonderfully vibrant, cheap prints. You can make your fabric découpage as wild and colourful or as sleek and sophisticated as you wish.

**You will need**
- Sponge craft brush
- PVA glue
- Odd remnants of fabric, cut into smallish pieces (preferably thin material, and ideally darker than the object you are covering)
- Scissors, large and small
- Your chosen object
- Ribbon, braid, pompoms, beads and any other trimmings

**1** Using either a sponge craft brush or your fingers, apply PVA glue to the back of the fabric. (The glue washes off skin easily.)

**2** Layer the fabric onto your chosen object one piece at a time, adding layers and overlapping edges until you're happy with the effect. Don't worry about being too neat – a few wrinkles will add to the charm.

**3** Leave to dry, then trim the edges with small, sharp scissors.

**4** Add your finishing touches, glueing on frills, bobbles, ribbons, pompoms, braid and ruching as you like. This is your chance to be really flamboyant!

# FOLDING NAPKINS

I always use proper linen napkins, never paper ones. I mix and match different fabrics and colours around the table, and think they add one of those small touches that just finishes off a table to perfection. Rather than placing them flat on the table, it's really easy to fold them into a wineglass – and something you can get your little helpers to do. Elanor Holland showed me how to make this variation on the classic kite fold.

**You will need**
- Square table napkin
- Wineglass
- Small sweet

**1** Take a square napkin that has been folded and ironed into quarters – these creases will help. Open it up and fold into a triangle with the long edge nearest you. If the napkin is patterned on only one side, make sure the pattern is on the inside of the triangle.

**2** Using your right hand, grasp the top layer of the napkin halfway down the left-hand side and raise it slightly. With your left hand, take the left-hand corner of the triangle underneath the raised edge and up to the top point. Lower the raised edge and you will now have 4 triangles sandwiched together. Swapping hands, repeat this step on the right-hand side. The overall shape you are left with is a square.

**3** Fold the left and right points of the top layer into the centre to create a kite shape. Turn the napkin over and do the same on the back.

**4** Roll up the long point and pop the napkin into a glass. All 4 corners of the napkin will flop outwards to look like flower petals. Place a sweet in the centre to look like the stamen.

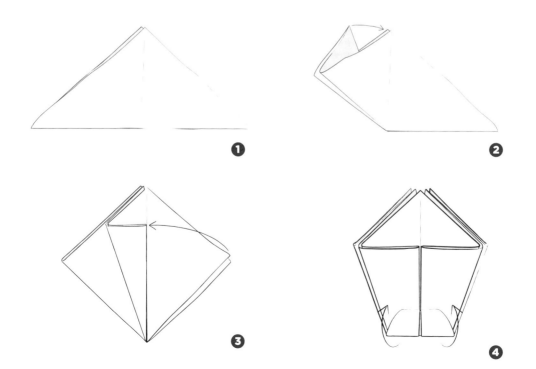

# MAKING A HERB GARDEN

It's never too soon to get children interested in gardening, and this is the perfect first project. A herb garden looks beautiful, smells fantastic and tastes delicious. It can be little or large, grown straight into your soil, or in pots, tins or baths. It's easy to manage too. Select the sunniest place in your garden, or on your balcony or windowsill, and don't forget to pick the herbs (and eat them) to keep the plants (and you) looking nice and healthy.

When choosing the herbs to put in your herb garden, make sure you ask the advice of a garden centre or plant expert about what will grow well together. My gardening friend Clemmie Hambro helped me. I learnt, for example, that mint is an overbearing little thug and will push all your other lovely herbs around, so keep that one on its own.

**You will need**
- Container, such as an old tin bath, sink, wooden trough or watering can; or several small plant pots, or even old baked bean tins with the labels removed (these look great on a windowsill)
- Hammer and nail (optional)
- Good multi-purpose compost
- Various pots of herbs
- Watering can

**1** Make sure your container has plenty of holes in the bottom for drainage. You can make these yourself if necessary by hammering a large nail through the base in several places.

**2** If your container is on the large size, place it in your chosen location (ideally a sunny but not too windy spot) before filling it because compost will make it very heavy to lug around. Fill the container with multi-purpose compost, but not right to the top: you'll need space to incorporate the rootball of the herbs into the soil.

**3** Plan out your herb garden, moving the pots around on top of the compost until you are happy with the arrangement and are sure that they have enough space to grow beside each other.

**4** Remove the herbs from their pots, and if the roots are looking a bit strangulated, gently tease them out a little with your fingers. Plant them into the soil and firm into position by pushing down the compost.

**5** Add a little more compost to level the surface, then water thoroughly.

# Light fantastic

## BESPOKE LAMPSHADE

I was completely empowered when lampshade designer Eileen Garsed showed me how to make a lampshade for the sitting room at Meadowgate, because with lampshades, it's my belief that you really do get what you pay for. And for most of us, the only way to get a bespoke look, with a fabric style and colour to match your room perfectly, is to make your own. The three main types of shade that Eileen makes are tailored, pleated and hard-framed. The last of these is probably the least complicated, so the instructions below are for making a simple hard-framed, drum lampshade. It's fairly straightforward to put together, but it is fiddly and requires real concentration, so perhaps best done when kids/family/friends are not distracting you!

**You will need**
- Fabric (silk, cotton, curtain fabric, or even your favourite wallpaper are all fine, but open-weave fabrics aren't great as dust and dirt will get into the exposed areas of the sticky backing material)
- Tape measure
- 2 wire-frame rings of same size, top one with inner ring to sit over light fitting
- Selapar (rigid, self-adhesive backing material, available in clear, white, gold and silver)
- Scissors (Eileen uses a rotary cutter and special ruler on a cutting board, but beginners don't need to invest in these items)
- Dress-making clamps or a few bulldog clips (as sold in stationers)
- Pencil
- 1-metre (3-ft) ruler for drawing the guideline
- 2 rolls double-sided sticky tape for use on fabric (3-mm & 12-mm widths; ordinary double-sided tape will *not* do as the bond is not strong enough)
- Pegs (optional)
- Braid or bias binding, to decorate (optional)

While most of the materials and equipment for this project can be bought from craft shops, sturdy wire frames and the special double-sided tape can be bought direct from Eileen (see page 214).

**1** Choose your fabric depending on what sort of light you want your lamp to give out. Red and yellow tones provide a warm glow, whereas greens and blues give a cooler light. I chose a purple fabric with some gold in it, (a) to give it warmth and (b) because it matched my pretty base. Make sure you iron the fabric if it's creased; no one likes a wrinkly lampshade.

**2** Measure the circumference of the lampshade rings, and add 2.5 cm (1 inch) to allow for the overlap. Make a note of the figure as this will be the length of the Selapar you need to cut.

**3** Now decide the depth you want your finished lampshade to be. Make a note of the figure.

**4** Cut your Selapar to the size you have just calculated: circumference + 2.5 cm (1 inch) long, and your chosen depth wide.

**5** Cut your fabric 1–1.5 cm (⅓–½ inch) longer than the Selapar. Lay the fabric face down on a work surface and, ideally, clamp it at one end while you draw a guideline down the length about 2.5 cm (1 inch) from the edge. This should follow the straight grain of the fabric and will be the line your Selapar will follow.

**6** Starting at the anchored end of the fabric, you now have to stick the Selapar onto the fabric next to the guideline. Peel back a small area of the film at one end of the Selapar and place the sticky surface down on the fabric. Working slowly and carefully, continue lifting off the film with one hand and smoothing the Selapar onto the fabric with the other. If you're doing this for the first time, it's easier if you get someone to help you.

**7** Stick a strip of the 3-mm double-sided tape down the length of the Selapar close to the edge, unwinding it from the roll as you go along. Repeat this step down the opposite length of the Selapar.

**8** Now stick a strip of the 12-mm double-sided tape along the fabric beside the narrow strip of tape on the Selapar. Repeat this step along the other side.

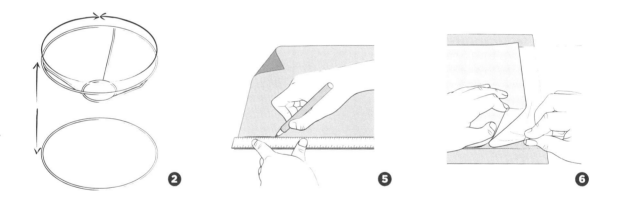

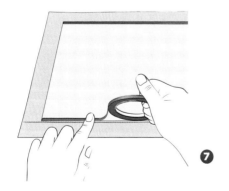

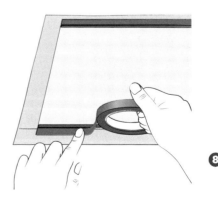

**9** Stick a strip of the 12-mm double-sided tape along one short end of the fabric next to the Selapar. Fold the extra fabric over the tape; this gives you a neatened edge for the seam. Stick another strip of 12-mm tape on top of that folded fabric. At the other short end, stick a strip of 12-mm tape on the fabric side. The idea is that these 2 strips will eventually overlap to form the seam of the shade, giving a very strong bond.

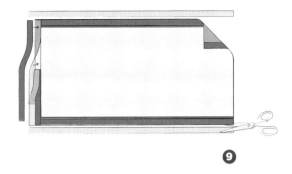

**10** Cut out the fabric up to tape on all sides.

**11** Now it's time to attach the stiffened fabric to the wire frame. If you're doing this for the first time, it's best to get someone to help you with this step. Lift up a short length of the film on the narrow tape and put the wire rings on the sticky surface. Carefully roll them along, pulling away the film as you do so. As the fabric attaches to the frame, you can use pegs to hold it in place if you wish. When you get to the overlap, peel the film off the 2 short strips of tape for the seam and press firmly together for a few minutes. When this is done you'll see that the shade is really taking shape.

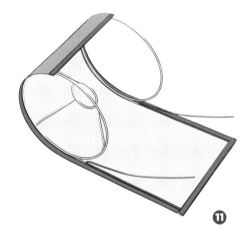

**12** Cut a 'V' halfway through the tape where each wire of the light fitting joins the outer ring. Peel the film off the sticky tape around the top of the frame and bend the fabric over the wire as neatly as possible. Repeat this around the bottom. The shade is now finished, but if you like, you can stick some braid or bias binding around the top and bottom edges on the outside.

**Tip**

If you want to revamp a boring lamp base or transform an existing lampshade, try covering it up with some lovely vintage fabric (see Découpage, page 132). Basically, you cut the fabric into little strips and stick them on with PVA glue. The result can be really lovely, and if you ever decide you want to revert to the original base, it's easy to remove the fabric.

# TEACUP CANDLE

Candles are such wonderful things. Their glow creates a certain atmosphere in a room that is impossible to recreate with electricity.

We have a great tradition of candle-making here in the UK, which is something I learnt only recently. We invented the modern production process and we spend an unbelievable £180 million a year on candles, so this isn't a craft you can ignore. Scented candles are particularly popular – I'd rather have a scented candle over an air freshener any day. But candles seem to be one of two things, either very expensive – and I've seen some that cost in excess of fifty quid in shops – or they're really cheap and last only an hour, like those ones you buy in bags of a hundred. Feels like the bargain of the century, but your money goes up in smoke just as quickly as they do.

Now the good news: candles are genuinely easy to make. There are lots of inexpensive kits out there that will supply you with everything you need, and it's a fairly quick process. I had a lesson from David Constable, a fantastic teacher who's been making candles for nearly half a century. He took me through the step-by-step process of making tall candles and teacup candles, using a couple of my own chipped teacups that I filled with wax. I hope you'll have a go at making these too.

**You will need**
- Teacup or similar container (ready-made moulds can be bought in craft shops or online, or use the ones that come with your candle-making kit)
- Wax (paraffin wax beads and beeswax, or old candles; beeswax acts as a hardening agent to give you a long, clean burn – use approx. 5 per cent beeswax to 95 per cent paraffin)
- Double-boiler (or one saucepan on top of another)
- Dye discs or liquid candle dye (optional)
- Container wick (paper- or metal-cored)
- Wick sustainer (the metal washer that is found at the base of a tea-light)
- Pair of pliers (for crimping)
- Essential oils (if you want to make scented candles)

All the materials needed for this project usually come with candle-making kits; if not, they can be bought from David Constable (see page 206).

1 First work out how much wax you will need: fill your teacup with water and measure the amount. Say it's 150 ml (5 fl oz), you will need the corresponding amount of wax, so 150 g (5 oz).

2 Put your wax ingredient(s) into the top pan of a double-boiler, and pour water into the bottom pan. (All wax has a flash point, so a double-boiler is essential to prevent it bursting into flames.)

3 If you want a coloured candle, add the dye now and melt it with the wax over a gentle heat. One dye disc will colour 2 kg (4½ lb) of wax, so you will need about one-tenth of a disc to colour a teacup candle, depending on how deep a shade you want.

4 Now prepare the wick. (A paper- or metal-cored container wick is essential as these have the rigidity to prevent them slumping into the molten wax and extinguishing themselves.) Cut the wick to a length 2 cm (¾ inch) longer than the teacup's depth. Now crimp the wick sustainer to one end of the cut wick and dip this ensemble into the prepared molten wax to prime it. Set aside.

5 If you want scented candles, choose an essential oil and do the following test to make sure it still smells pleasant when heated. Pour some oil into a teaspoon or incense burner, heat until it vaporises, then take a sniff. If you like it, melt 1 tablespoon wax and add a few drops of the oil to it. Stir well, then pour the mixture into an eggcup or similar small container and leave to set. Flip out the wax. If there is any oil left in the eggcup, or it has collected in a blister at the bottom of the wax, it is *not* suitable for your candle. You *must* use an oil that stays in suspension within the wax. If your oil passes this test, add 1 teaspoon oil to 100 g (4 oz) of molten wax and stir well. I chose pine, which is traditionally used for relaxing muscles and increasing energy – perfect for my bathroom.

6 Pour the wax into your teacup all in one go. Once a fine skin has developed on the surface of the wax, gently push your primed wick through it in the centre of the teacup so that the wick sustainer sits at the bottom of the cup.

7 After approximately 30 minutes, you will notice a well forming in the top of the wax as it cools and contracts. Break the skin of the well, taking care to keep the wick in the centre of the cup. Do this every 20 minutes until the wax has fully congealed. Now reheat your remaining wax and fill the wax-well. For larger containers, you might have to repeat this topping-up process a few times.

8 After one day your candle will be ready to burn.

# Upholstery

I'm a massive fan of picking up second-hand chairs and sofas at auctions, antiques stores, markets, reclamation yards... generally wherever I find them. For me, it doesn't matter that they have a bit of wear and tear because any damage is normally reflected in the price tag, or at least I make it reflect the amount I'm willing to pay by working out how much it might cost me to repair on my own or at my upholsterer's. It's worth doing some research about these costs in advance, as it could give you the confidence you need to buy a good, solid, old piece of furniture that, with a bit of tarting up, will be just as good as new. That's why upholstery is one of my favourite crafts: it's all about recycling, reusing and breathing new life into something, rather than chucking it out because it's a bit rough around the edges.

I have been known to do a bit of DIY upholstery, but I knew my 200-year-old Regency chair needed more than my basic skills could offer, so I took it to Fraser McKay, a local Devon upholsterer who uses traditional methods and natural materials to treat and transform old furniture. He gave my chair a new lease of life and it is now in the master bedroom at Meadowgate.

You can do basic upholstery jobs at home (see overleaf), but if you're fearful of tackling an antique, take it to a local upholsterer who will give it the TLC it deserves. It might seem expensive, but by getting a chair reupholstered you could be adding another 80 years to its life, giving you something to pass onto your children, and their children after that.

# RESTORING A DROP-IN SEAT PAD

Upholstery can seem frightening to those who've never tried it, but Fraser McKay is an expert, and his steps for revitalising a footstool or chair with a drop-in seat pad are really straightforward. They apply to a modern stool or chair, without webbing.

**You will need**
- Old seat pad
- Ripping chisel
- Mallet
- Foam, 2.5 cm (1 inch) thick
- Felt-tip pen
- Bread knife
- Can of spray adhesive
- Cotton felt
- Calico
- Tape measure
- 10-mm tacks (for temporary tacking)
- Tack hammer
- 6-mm tacks, or staple gun and 8-mm staples (for permanent tacking)
- Pincers
- Sharp scissors
- Upholstery fabric for top cover
- Black cotton base cloth

All the materials used in this project can be obtained from your local upholsterer.

**1** Strip out the old seat pad using a ripping chisel and a mallet, being careful to work with the grain of wood.

**2** Place the stripped frame over a piece of foam and draw around it with a felt-tip pen, leaving about 7 mm (¼ inch) overhang all round.

**3** Cut out the foam using a bread knife and glue it to the frame using a spray adhesive.

**4** Spread a piece of cotton felt over the foam; this will give comfort and shape, and make the seat more hard-wearing. With one hand on the seat, tease the excess felt away with the other hand. When finished, you should be able to see the edge of the foam under the felt.

**5** Now make the calico cover. (This helps create the shape of the seat and will absorb any stains, thus helping the top cover to last longer.) Measure around the seat from one inside edge of the underside frame to the other. Do this both widthways and lengthways to ensure you have enough calico to work with.

**6** Lay the calico over the felt and turn the seat over. Pull the calico up, not too tightly, ensuring that the felt does not hang over the edge of the wood. Remember, this is a drop-in seat, so it has to fit into the original frame. If you have too much felt on the edge, just tease it out until you can see the wood edge under the foam. Temporary tack using 10-mm tacks, finishing about 4 cm (1½ inches) from each corner. All the fullness in the calico must be at the corners.

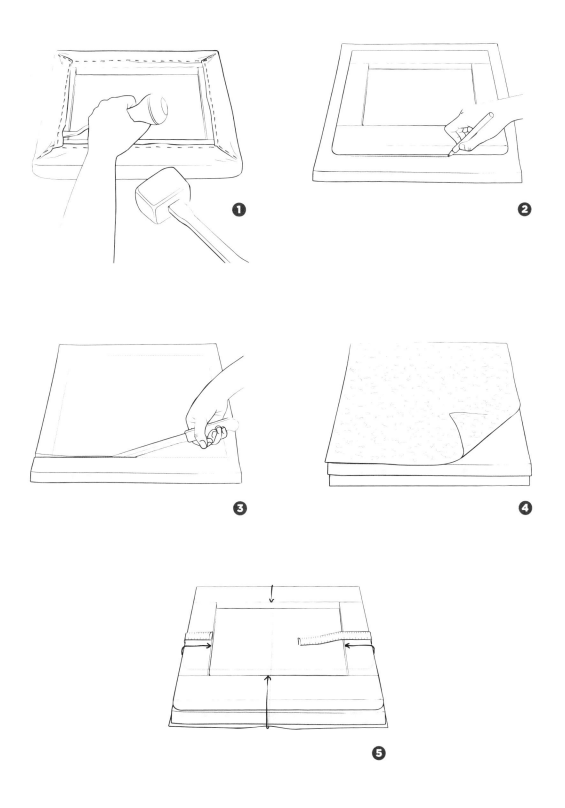

**7** Working from the centre of one side, remove the temporary tacks and pull the calico tight, ensuring that the cotton felt is not pulled over the wooden edge. Insert permanent 6-mm tacks or staples about 2 cm (¾ inch) from the edge, stopping 4 cm (1½ inches) from the corner. Repeat this process on the other 3 sides.

**8** On one side insert permanent tacks or staples up to the corner. The calico will almost have formed its own pleat, like a hospital corner on a bed (A). Cut out the excess calico, then permanently tack or staple down the pleat (B). Repeat this process with the remainder of the calico at the corner until you have a neat finish (C). Repeat for all the remaining corners.

**9** Cut out a piece of your top fabric, measuring as before with the calico, but this time make a mark at the centre of each edge and on the frame edges

too. Line up the fabric marks with the marks on the frame and temporary tack, as you did in step 6, ensuring you keep the thread lines of the fabric straight.

**10** Fix the top fabric to the frame as you did with the calico in steps 6 and 7, this time inserting the permanent tacks or staples about 4 cm (1½ inches) from the edge.

**11** Now do the corners as you did in step 8.

**12** Cut a piece of base cloth to size and lay it over the underside of the seat, covering the tacks or staples. Turn under the base cloth about 1.5 cm (½ inch) all round and fix in place with permanent tacks or staples about 1.5 cm (½ inch) from the edge.

**13** Replace the seat pad in its frame and the job is complete.

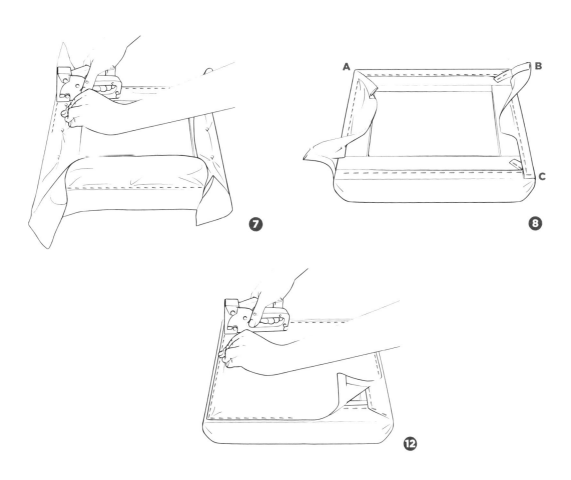

# Crafts to take your time over

## SCREEN-PRINTING WALLPAPER

I learnt to screen-print with a talented young printmaker named Emma Molony, and I chose my downstairs loo as the canvas. Being so small, it wouldn't break my budget to have handmade wallpaper on every wall.

Screen-printing is like stencilling in that the ink goes through only the open areas of the design onto the surface below. It involves more complicated equipment than stencilling, but with a bit of time and planning, you honestly can do it from home and save yourself pots of money to boot. And the best bit is that you can print anything onto wallpaper – a family photo, a particular colour scheme, or even words from your favourite book. Making it something personal to you is what's fun. And if you don't have the time, there are artisans and wallpaper-makers out there who'll do it for you, creating a personalised wall covering that will last the distance.

You can buy screens for screen-printing from a craft or art shop, or you can have a go at making one yourself from an old window frame and some fabric stapled tightly to the edges of the frame. The best fabric is a monofilament polyester, such as chiffon, nylon or polyester.

Once you've got your screen, all you need is some paint, a roll of cheap lining paper (it's best to start with the cheap stuff), your design, lots of space to work in, a large, flat table and you're ready to go.

## You will need

- Lining paper
- Watered-down emulsion paint
- Large paintbrush
- Sheets of newsprint
- Pencil
- Scissors or craft knife
- Ink (you can use an acrylic paint and screen-print medium, such as those from www.daler-rowney. com/content/system-3-acrylics, or Selectasine dye and binder, from www.selectasine.com)
- Screen (see introduction opposite)
- Brown parcel tape
- Squeegee slightly wider than your design
- Sheets of scrap paper
- Something to prop up your screen (e.g. a roll of tape)
- Spatulas, for pouring ink and scraping off the squeegee and screen
- Garden hose or bucket and sponge (for washing your screen)

**1** Prime your lining paper with a background colour of watered-down emulsion paint, otherwise the paper will discolour over time. Leave to dry.

**2** Design your stencil. Draw your pattern onto thin paper, such as newsprint, remembering that the ink will print only in the gaps of the design. Use scissors or a craft knife to cut out the areas of the design that will print.

**3** Mix up your ink according to the manufacturer's instructions.

**4** Prepare the screen. Stick strips of brown parcel tape around the inside edge of the screen to create a window smaller than your stencil and to prevent the ink from squeezing out of the corners of the screen and stencil. Make sure this inner frame is firmly stuck down to avoid leaks.

**5** The next step is to attach the stencil to the screen. Place your stencil on a wipeable surface and place the screen over it.

**6** Pour plenty of ink along one edge of the screen, then pull the squeegee firmly and evenly across the mesh of the screen at a 45-degree angle. This pushes the ink through the cut-out parts of your stencil. When you lift the screen your stencil should be attached to it. If not, you can tape the corners of the stencil to the underside of the screen to secure it.

**7** Wipe down the work surface. Prop the screen up so it's not touching anything and use the squeegee to lightly pull the ink back over it. This is called 'flooding' and is very important because you're preparing the screen for printing and also ensuring that the small amount of ink left in the mesh after printing doesn't dry and block your design. You'll need to flood each time you print.

**8** Now you're ready to print. You can do this on scrap paper a few times to experiment with the pressure of pulling the squeegee and to be sure the design is printing well before you try it on your wallpaper. When you're happy with the result, place your primed paper on the table and prop the screen over it so that it's not touching the paper until you're ready to print. As in step 6, lay your screen flat on the paper and pull the squeegee firmly across it, squeezing the ink through your design on the mesh and onto your wallpaper. Prop the screen up and remember to flood it, as in step 7. Then move the screen to the next position, taking care not to smudge the just-printed design; you might need print alternate gaps to allow the fresh work to dry.

**9** If you want to print your design in different colours, place the screen on newspaper and clean off the unwanted colour with a damp sponge. Keep sponging onto clean newspaper, effectively printing all the ink out of the screen. This must be done carefully as the paper stencil is very delicate. When the screen is clean, apply the new colour as described in step 6. When you have finished, take the screen outside and clean it thoroughly with a hosepipe or bucket of water and sponge. It's important to avoid ink drying into the screen and blocking the mesh.

# MOSAIC TABLE

I have to admit that when we were planning which crafts to feature, mosaic wasn't the one I was most looking forward to. I didn't think I liked it much – too many history lessons about the Romans when I really wanted to be learning about Mary Queen of Scots. Then I met Kaffe Fassett. He has created an amazing mosaic within his front porch, and I fell in love with it. And by the time I'd seen the garden and fantastic mosaic objects created by Candace Bahouth it was official – I was head over heels.

The great thing about mosaic is that it's both entirely decorative and immensely practical. As I learnt from mosaic expert Emma Biggs, it's also really easy to get started, so once you've mastered the basic skills, the opportunities to make beautiful things are endless.

The art of mosaic-making dates back thousands of years to ancient Greece, but it was the Romans who first brought it to Britain around the first century AD. It's still commonly seen on floors, walls and objects both inside and out. Basically, there are very few surfaces you can't stick bits to, and that's why mosaic provides a great opportunity to let your imagination soar.

You can mosaic with pretty much anything – pebbles, shells, bits of marble, mirror or glass, and all sorts of ceramics. I've got loads of old chipped bits and bobs that I've collected over the years from junk shops and markets, and I've found that making mosaics gives you a much more positive attitude to the children breaking things.

But first things first: you need to decide what you want to create. My best advice is to start with something small and simple, and be patient – you know what they say, Rome wasn't built in a day!

**You will need**
- Tabletop to mosaic
- Paper and pencil
- Craft knife
- Tesserae (bits of broken pottery, glass, pebbles or shells, or ready-made glass/ceramic squares produced specially for mosaic work)
- Tile nippers and/or glass cutters or wheeled nippers
- Small hammer (optional)
- Old towel
- Protective goggles
- Latex-based adhesive
- Small palette knife
- Grout
- Rubber gloves
- Grouting squeegee
- Sponge
- Damp cloth (the old towel is ideal)
- Fine sandpaper, if necessary
- Lint-free cloth

**OPPOSITE:**
The inspirational mosaic in Kaffe Fassett's porch.

**1** First, choose a surface you'd like to mosaic. The easiest surface to work on is wood, and my small round tabletop was ideal for a first attempt.

**2** Next, sketch out your design on a piece of paper and think about the colours you want to use. Try not to over-complicate the design on your first attempt. A simple, well-done mosaic will look just as lovely as a really detailed one. For my tabletop, I chose a central motif of a red heart against a background of blue-green tiles, with an outer border of blue and white.

**3** When you're happy with your design, sketch it on to the tabletop, then score the surface with a craft knife. This gives a 'key' to help the adhesive and tiles stick better.

**4** Now choose your mosaic materials, bearing in mind the end use of your creation. For my tabletop I used old broken plates to give me a pretty ceramic edge and new glass tiles in the centre to provide the even surface needed for a table.

**5** The way you cut your materials depends on what they are made from. Tile nippers are used to cut tiles and crockery pieces, while glass cutters or wheeled nippers, which have a gentler action, are used on mirror and glass tiles. For really thick bits or larger pieces of tesserae, some people use a little hammer to break them down before clipping. To do this, pop them under an old towel first to stop rogue shards flying around, and do wear protective goggles. A word of warning, though – this technique can create unpredictable, very sharp and uneven cuts. You really are better off using tile nippers, where the results can be more controlled.

**6** Once all the mosaic pieces are ready, you can experiment a bit at a time with where you want to place the tiles. It's rather like a jigsaw in that you are looking for the most obvious fit. When you're happy with the arrangement, you can go on to the next step.

**7** Here comes the sticky part. If, like me, you're making a tabletop using materials of different thicknesses, lay the thickest pieces first, then put extra adhesive behind the thinner pieces to bring them up to the same level. This will ensure you get an even surface. Starting at the borders of a tile, 'butter' it with a small amount of adhesive, then carefully press it down. If any adhesive squidges out, remove it immediately before moving on to the next tile or it will spoil the appearance. You need to leave a 3-mm (⅛ inch) gap between the pieces for the grouting. Once all the tiles are stuck down, they must be left to set for 24 hours.

**8** Mix the grout according to the instructions on the packet. (You can use coloured grout if that works better for the design.) Wearing rubber gloves, spread it over the mosaic by hand, filling in the spaces between the pieces. Carefully sweep the squeegee across the surface to remove excess grout, then leave it for about 30 minutes to begin setting. Gently wipe the surface with a damp sponge to remove any final traces of grout on the tiles, then cover with a damp cloth and leave to set completely. The more slowly it dries, the stronger the finish.

**9** Once the grout is completely dry, clean the mosaic with a damp cloth. If there is any dried-on grout, remove it carefully with fine sandpaper and wipe down again. Once you're happy with the surface, buff the mosaic with a lint-free cloth.

# RAG RUG

If, like me, you're reluctant to throw anything away, here's a great project for recycling old clothes, and it makes a lovely treat for your toes first thing in the morning. This rag rug, with its jazzy leaf design, was made by textile artist Debbie Siniska, who's been involved in traditional crafts for many years. There are various methods of rag-rugging, but the one used here is very straightforward: it produces a shaggy surface rather than a looped one, and is both quick and wonderfully relaxing to do. The rug is worked in six separate squares that are then sewn together and hemmed. Once you've mastered the basic technique, you'll be turning out rugs like there's no tomorrow.

**You will need**
- Hessian (10-oz weight)
- Tape measure or ruler
- Felt-tip pen
- Cardboard template
- Old clothes (T-shirts or fine woollies are ideal)
- Scissors
- Cutting gauge (a piece of wood with a groove along one side of it, optional)
- Bodger (a grasping tool with a sprung jaw)
- Sturdy needle
- Strong thread

The equipment for this project can be bought online from Debbie Siniska (see page 216) or from craft shops.

**1** Cut out a 25 x 25-cm (10 x 10-inch) piece of hessian. Mark out a 20 x 20-cm (8 x 8-inch) square on it using a felt-tip pen.

**2** Cut a leaf-shaped template out of cardboard, making sure that it will fit inside the outlined square. Place it on the hessian and draw around it with the felt-tip pen.

**3** Cut some old clothes into strips 1.5 cm (½ inch) wide. Now cut these into shorter pieces (tabs) about 8 cm (3 inches) long. You can do this quickly and easily by winding a strip of fabric around a cutting gauge and cutting along the groove. Alternatively, you can wind the strip around two fingers and cut between the gap.

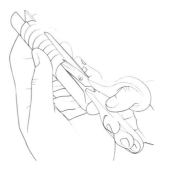

**4** Begin to work the surface of the hessian using a bodger. This tool has a sprung jaw that catches hold of the fabric tabs and pulls them through the hessian. Starting within the leaf outline (it doesn't matter where), push the bodger into the top side of the hessian and bring it up 3 threads forward.

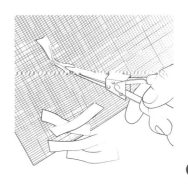

**5** Open the sprung jaw of the bodger and grab one end of a fabric tab. Pull the tab halfway through the two holes and then release the sprung jaw.

**6** For the next stitch, push the bodger into the same hole as the last stitch, then on into a new hole to catch hold of the next tab of fabric. Continue in this way until you have covered the whole surface.

**7** Turn the hem under all round the square and stitch in place.

**8** Make 5 more squares in the same way. Arrange them as you wish, then turn them over, butt up the edges and overstitch them together to make your 6-squared rug.

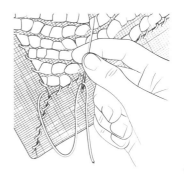

# Crochet

Crochet is arguably easier than knitting because all you need is a crochet hook and a continuous length of yarn, and you work just one stitch at a time. It's certainly easy to learn, simple to do and really quick, as I discovered when I met crochet designer Erika Knight.

Starting with just a slip-knot, you make a series of loops or chains. This gives you a foundation chain, and from this you make the first row. There are just a few basic stitches, which can combine to create a variety of fabrics – firm and hard-edged, soft and supple, intricately detailed, or light and open. And you can crochet with almost anything from traditional fine cotton and commercially bought yarns to leather, rags and string.

Crochet can be worked in rows or rounds to make either flat fabrics or shaped ones. Erika showed me how to make some very simple and practical boxes, and I was thrilled with the result.

First, though, let's start with some basics to get you going. You'll be hooked in no time!

# HOW TO CROCHET

**You will need**
- Crochet hook
- Ball of yarn
- Tapestry needle (for weaving loose end of yarn into finished work)

## HOLDING THE HOOK
The easiest way to hold the hook is either like a pencil or a knife – whichever feels most comfortable.

## START WITH A SLIP-KNOT
Leaving an end of about 15 cm (6 inches), make a loop, then insert the hook and catch the ball end of the yarn with it. Pull the yarn through the loop, then pull both ends of the yarn to tighten the knot.

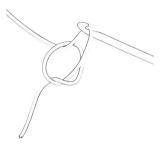

## HOLDING THE YARN
The yarn is held in the opposite hand to the hook. Most people choose to wrap it around the fingers, perhaps making an additional wrap around the little finger. (Erika favours wrapping the yarn around her little finger, over the next two fingers, and catching it with her forefinger so that her middle finger controls the yarn.) Choose whichever method works best for you. You just need to hold the yarn firmly enough so that when you draw the hook around the yarn, it stays in the lip of the hook.

## MAKING A CHAIN STITCH
With the hook in the loop you've just made, catch the yarn and pull it through (A & B). Keep repeating this step to make a row of chains (C). You have now made a foundation chain (also called a foundation row). Each chain counts as 1 stitch, but the working chain (the one the hook is in) is never counted and neither is the slip-knot at the start. When you count the chains, make sure they are not twisted.

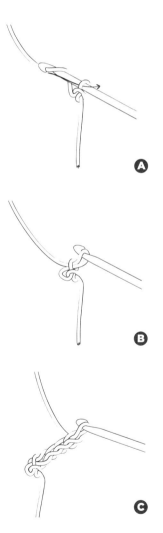

## DOUBLE CROCHET STITCH

This stitch, abbreviated as 'dc', creates a dense yet flexible fabric, which is ideal for hard-wearing, strong textile. It's the easiest of all crochet fabrics to make.

**1** When you've made a foundation chain with the number of chains you require, insert the hook into the 2nd chain from the hook. Wrap the yarn around the hook and pull it through the chain. There are now 2 loops on the hook.

**2** Wrap the yarn around the hook and draw it through both loops on the hook. This leaves 1 loop on the hook and completes the first double crochet.

**3** Insert the hook through the next chain and pull the yarn through both loops on the hook.

**4** Repeat this step with each of the remaining chains to complete the 1st row.

**5** To start any subsequent rows of double crochet, turn the work so that the loop on the hook is at the right-hand edge. Make a loose chain to take the yarn up to the correct height by drawing the yarn through the loop on the hook. This is 1 turning chain (t-ch) and counts as 1st dc in the new row.

**6** Miss the 1st stitch at the base of the t-ch and insert the hook through both loops at the top of the next stitch in the row. Now work a double crochet into the the next stitch and every stitch after that to the end of the row, including the turning chain.

Now you can crochet!

### FASTENING OFF

When you have finished your piece, complete the final stitch, then cut the working yarn and pull it through the last loop on the hook. Tighten the yarn to close the loop and weave the loose end into the back of the work with a tapestry needle.

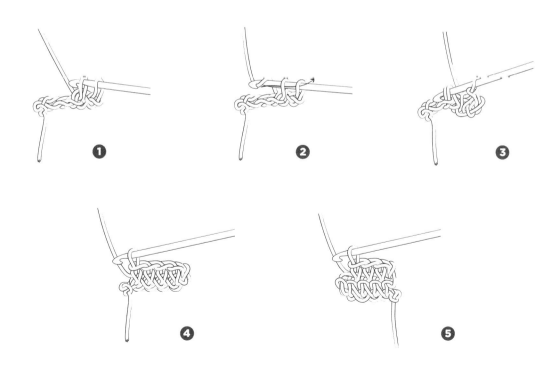

# CROCHET BOX

Here's a great project to get started – a simple crochet box that is both cheap and easy to make. Depending on what size you make it, the box can be used to store all sorts of things around the home – toiletries, pens and pencils, shoes, cutlery... It could even cover a plant pot, or hold all your yarns and hooks for new crochet projects.

The box is worked in basic double crochet using coloured garden string, and is trimmed in a contrast colour or texture. The instructions below are for a box 15 cm (6 inches) square and a rectangular box 30 x 21 x 12 cm (12 x $8^{1}/_{4}$ x $4^{3}/_{4}$ inches) – the rectangle instructions appear in square brackets – but the pattern can be made to any size you want by adding more stitches and rows.

**You will need**
- Large ball of garden twine or parcel string, or oddments of yarn from your stash
- Contrasting colour yarn (optional)
- 1 x 5 mm crochet hook (US size H/8)

**TENSION**
The box has a tension (stitch size) of 11.5 stitches and 13 rows to 10 cm (4 inches) measured over double crochet, but working to an exact tension is not essential. However, it is important to create a nice firm fabric that will hold the shape well. Make the sides and ends of the box first, following the instructions given. Then make the base, adding or subtracting from the number of stitches recommended until the depth of the piece matches the width of the ends.

Note: Measurements are approximate as different types of string (parcel, garden, etc.) will result in a different tension/size.

**BOX SIDES (MAKE 2)**
**Foundation chain:** Leaving a long loose end of string, make 17 [34] chains.

**Row 1:** Work 1dc into 2nd chain from hook, 1dc into each of remaining chains. Turn.

**Row 2:** 1 ch (this counts as 1st dc of row, so work it loosely), miss 1st dc and work 1dc into next dc, then work 1dc into each of remaining dc, work last dc into 1-ch at edge. Turn. There are 16 [33] stitches in the row.

Repeat row 2 until work measures 14 [11] cm or $5^{1}/_{2}$ [$4^{1}/_{4}$] inches from foundation chain edge.

Fasten off.

## BOX BASE (MAKE 1)
**Foundation chain:** Leaving a long loose end of string, make 17 [34] chains.

Work rows 1 and 2 as for box sides.

Repeat row 2 on these 16 [33] stitches until work measures 15 [21] cm or 6 [8¼] inches from foundation chain edge.

Fasten off.

## MAKING UP
Using a tapestry needle, weave any loose ends into the work.

Oversew the ends and sides together to make a box shape. Oversew the box base to the sides and ends in the same way.

## EDGING
Using a contrast colour or texture of yarn or string, work a row of dc all around the top of the box.

Fasten off.

Weave in any loose ends.

## BOX ENDS (MAKE 2)
**Foundation chain:** Leaving a long loose end of string, make 17 [24] chains.

Work rows 1 and 2 as for box sides.

Repeat row 2 on these 16 [23] stitches until there are the same number of rows as on sides.

Fasten off.

happy people

# QUILTED PATCHWORK CUSHION COVER

As if you hadn't guessed, I'm obsessed with quilts. I love patchworks, plain stitch, eiderdowns, all of them. They are wonderful heirlooms and I'll be passing mine down to my children, even though they're boys.

I look at websites selling quilts the way others sit glued to costume dramas on television, so you can imagine my excitement when I was offered the chance to meet Jo Colwill at her quilting workshop in Cornwall. Jo is passionate about textiles, and she's been designing and making her own quilts for over 20 years.

A quilt is a bit like a sandwich – three layers are stitched together, with the bottom being a backing layer of soft fabric, the middle being a thermal layer for warmth, and the top being the decorative layer with all the detail. The great thing is that you can use oddments of fabric, old clothes or other recycled scraps of material, whatever you have to hand. That's the beauty of patchwork – it's an amalgamation of fabric pieces often loaded with memories, and the detail and intricacy will have you studying it for hours.

For Meadowgate, Jo helped me design and make a quilt for the children's bedroom using the appliqué method, which means you sew on shapes, folding under the edges.

Making any large quilt or patchwork requires a tremendous amount of time and commitment. It's not something you can do in a week (unless you give up everything else in life, including sleeping), but starting off on something small, such as a patchwork cushion cover, is a tremendous joy, and by building up a bit of skill and enthusiasm, perhaps you'll eventually want to take on the challenge of a full quilt.

**You will need**
- Ruler
- Pencil and paper
- Scissors
- Selection of fabrics in similar weights
- Pins
- Tape measure
- Needle or sewing machine
- Neutral-coloured thread
- Calico
- Wadding
- Water-erasable pen or tailor's chalk (optional), for drawing diagonal lines
- Plain fabric, for borders and back of cover
- Cushion pad 25 cm (10 inches) square

Note: It's easy to make the cover in different sizes. Just increase or reduce the number of patchwork squares needed to cover your cushion, remembering to allow for a border of 4 cm (1½ inches) around them. Cut the calico and wadding to match your patchwork piece. For the border you need 4 strips 4 cm (1½ inches) wide: 2 of these should be 1.5 cm (½ inch) longer than the patchwork, and 2 should be 5 cm (2 inches) longer than the patchwork.

1 Cut out a paper template measuring 6 cm (2½ inches) square. Place this on a a mixed selection of fabrics and cut out 25 squares. Lay them face up in 5 rows of 5 squares, moving the different fabrics around until you have an arrangement you are happy with. It is good to choose a variety of patterns – prints, stripes, dots, flowers, plains.

2 Pin the fabrics together in strips of 5 squares, taking a seam allowance of 5 mm (¼ inch). Hand-sew or machine-stitch the squares together, then press the seams open and closed alternately, as shown opposite. This will make it easier to cross-match the rows in step 3.

3 Pin the 5 strips together to make a large square, matching the seams accurately and taking a 5-mm (¼-inch) seam allowance. Sew the strips together and press the seams open. You now have the patchworked front of your cover.

4 Cut a piece of calico and a piece of wadding to the same size as the patchwork. Sit the wadding on the calico, then place the patchwork face up on the wadding. Tack the three layers together. Pin or draw diagonal lines across the patchwork, making sure they go through the points where 4 squares meet. These are your quilting lines. Tack together and remove the pins. Machine-stitch along these lines, through all 3 layers, then remove the tacking threads.

**5** For the borders, cut 2 strips of plain fabric measuring 4 x 26 cm (1½ x 10¼ inches) and 2 strips measuring 4 x 32 cm (1½ x 12½ inches). Pin the 2 shorter strips to the sides of the patchwork front, taking a 5-mm (¼-inch) seam. Stitch in place and press the seam open. Pin the 2 longer strips along the top and bottom of the patchwork front and stitch in place. Press the seams open. Trim away any excess wadding or calico.

**6** To make the back of the cover, cut out 2 pieces of plain fabric measuring 32 x 21 cm (12½ x 10¼ inches). Fold over a 5-mm (¼-inch) double hem on 1 longer side of each rectangle. Pin in place, press and stitch. Overlap the 2 rectangles by 9 cm (3½ inches), with the hemmed edges towards the centre. This should make a square the same size as the front of the cover. Pin the 2 rectangles together through the overlap to hold them together.

**7** Place the front and back cover pieces right sides together. Pin around all 4 sides, taking a 5-mm (¼-inch) seam allowance, then stitch. Run the machine back and forth across the overlap a few times to reinforce the opening. Remove pins.

**8** Clip the corners diagonally to reduce the bulk. Turn the cover right side out and insert the cushion pad through the envelope opening on the back.

**Tip**
Instead of quilting diagonally across the squares, you could sew old mother-of-pearl buttons at the points where the squares meet, or hand-quilt the piece, using heart and flower shapes.

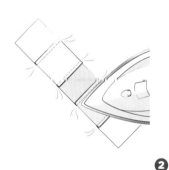

**2**

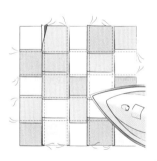

**3**

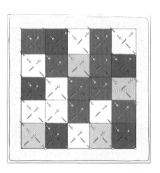

**4**

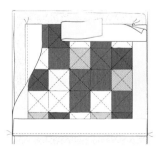

**5**

**7**

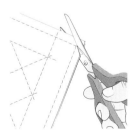

**8**

# Knitting

My granny tried to teach me to knit when I was little, but gave up on me because I was left-handed. For years I envied knitters, thinking I could never learn, but since meeting Suzie Johnson, a knitting designer who owns The Wool Sanctuary, and learning the basics, I'm getting the hang of it. Knitting does take patience and some concentration, but the pleasure you get from creating something as comforting as a jumper or scarf is immense.

Knitting used to be an essential skill for every mother or grandmother, but in the real olden days the knitting was actually done by men, and the first knitters were Arabian fishermen who used to knit their nets. More recently, knitting has moved in and out of fashion: it made it to the pages of *Vogue* in the 1970s, while the 1990s saw it cast aside by anyone not drawing their pension, but today the craft has attracted a host of Hollywood wool-lovers, including Julia Roberts, Madonna and Russell Crowe (allegedly).

Trendy knitting shops have sprung up everywhere, and never has there been a greater selection of beautifully coloured yarns. Also, the variety of fibres is astounding, including alpaca, cashmere, mohair, cotton and silk, and even soya and bamboo!

The great thing about knitting is that you can do it virtually anywhere – on the bus on the way to work, during your lunch break, in the pub with friends... It's the ultimate portable hobby.

If, like I was, you're fearful of picking up needles for the first time in ages, or have never tried before, do not be afraid. Pluck up your courage and follow the basic steps to cast on and do the knit stitch. If I can, anyone can...

# HOW TO KNIT

There are entire books (and lives) devoted to this craft, but on these humble pages are the four basics to get you started: casting on, knit stitch, purl stitch and casting off. The instructions below are for a right-handed knitter, so you can reverse them if you are left-handed. That said, a lot of left-handers knit right-handed, so it's best to experiment with what is most comfortable.

Note: If you're following a pattern, the instructions will tell you how many stitches to cast on. If you are just knocking up some squares for practice, then look at the paper band on your ball of yarn for information on your tension square. This will tell you how many stitches over how many rows using which size needles it takes to make a 10-cm (4-inch) square. This shows what your tension needs to be to create a garment of the right size.

## You will need
- Yarn
- Knitting needles
- Scissors
- Patience

## START WITH A SLIP-KNOT
The slip-knot is the very first 'stitch' that you cast onto your knitting needle. You should leave a long, loose end (at least 15 cm/6 inches) so that it can either be darned in or used to sew the seam.

**1** Wind the yarn twice around two fingers on your left hand to make a circle of yarn as shown below. With the knitting needle, pull a loop of the yarn attached to the ball through the yarn circle on your fingers.

**2** Pull both ends of the yarn to tighten the slip-knot on the needle. You are now ready to cast on.

## CASTING ON
There are a number of ways to cast on, but this cable technique is one of the easier methods.

**1** Hold the needle with the slip-knot in your left hand. Put the tip of the right-hand needle into the stitch on the left-hand needle, making a cross. The right needle should be behind the left needle.

**2** Using your right hand, pick up the yarn and take it under and around the point of the right needle. Pull the yarn just tight enough to secure it.

**3** Bring the tip of the right needle with the yarn wrapped around it through the stitch on the left needle and towards you.

**4** The yarn needs to be pulled through enough to be placed on the left needle. To do this, use the left needle to pick up the loop, slipping the right needle away. You should now have 2 stitches.

**5** To cast on the remaining stitches, put the tip of the right needle between the last two stitches (note, not into a stitch) and repeat steps 1–3. Keep repeating step 4 until you have the desired number of stitches on your left needle. Congratulations, you have just learnt to cast on.

 **1**

 **2**

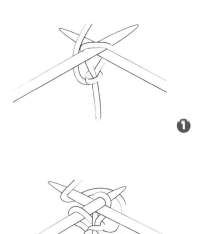

## KNIT STITCH

Now you've cast on, you're well on your way to knitting your first row. This is the basic knit stitch.

**1** You knit from left to right, so holding the knitting in your left hand, insert the tip of the right needle into the back of the first stitch and behind the left-hand needle.

**2** Taking the yarn with your right hand, bring it around and over the right needle.

**3** Bring the tip of the right needle and the yarn you have just wrapped around it through the stitch on the left needle and towards you.

**4** Slip the loop you have just knitted into off the left needle and onto the right. Well done, you have just knitted your first stitch.

**5** Repeat steps 1–4 until the end of the row.

Only another 40 rows to go and it'll feel like you're getting somewhere! That's what Suzie said to me. She was cruel saying that, but I swear you do get faster.

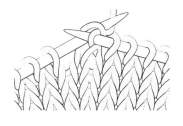

## PURL STITCH

The purl stitch involves holding the yarn at the front of your work, so it's the opposite of what you did for knit stitch.

**1** With the yarn at the front, put the tip of the right needle through the front of the first stitch on the left needle so that your right needle is at the front.

**2** Take the yarn over and around the tip of the right needle.

**3** Take the loop you have just wrapped back through the stitch and onto the right needle. You have now purled your first stitch!

**4** Repeat steps 1–3 until the end of the row.

## CASTING OFF

Once you've finished your piece of knitting, you need to cast off securely so that your stitches don't unravel. You can cast off on a purl row or a knit row. The instructions below are for a knit row. For a purl row, just read purl instead of knit.

**1** Knit the first 2 stitches from your left needle.

**2** Using the tip of your left needle, pick up the first stitch that you have just knitted on your right needle and pull it over the top of the second, then off the needle.

**3** Knit the next stitch and repeat step 2. Continue in this way until you are left with 1 stitch.

**4** Cut the yarn, leaving an end of around 10 cm (4 inches), which will be sewn in later, and thread the end through this final stitch. You've done it!

**1**

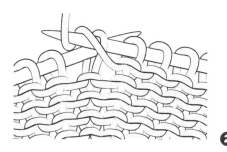

**2**

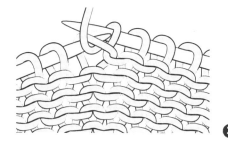

**3**

### KIRSTIE'S DRAUGHT EXCLUDER

A kit for the draught excluder I made on the first series of *Homemade Home* is available from The Wool Sanctuary (see page 213). But I wanted to start you off with something a little simpler, so on the next few pages are Suzie's instructions for a knitted tea cosy and an egg cosy, both guaranteed to brighten anyone's morning.

# KNITTED TEA COSY

## You will need
- 2 x 50-g balls DK, pale pink (Yarn A)
- 1 x 50-g ball DK, green (Yarn B)
- 1 x 50-g ball DK, purple (Yarn C)
- 1 x 50-g ball DK, pink (Yarn D)
- 1 x 50-g ball DK, blue (Yarn E)
- 1 x 50-g ball DK, brown (Yarn F)
- 1 pair of 4 mm (US size 6) needles
- Stitch holder

## Abbreviations
| | |
|---|---|
| DK | Double knit |
| G-st | Garter stitch (which means you knit every row) |
| K | Knit |
| K2tog | Knit 2 together |
| P | Purl |
| Sts | Stitches |
| St-st | Stocking stitch (you knit a row, then purl a row, and continue in this way) |

## Note
Both the tea cosy and the egg cosy (see page 178) are worked in garter stitch. There are only 6 purl rows in the pattern, and these create the roof edges on both cosies.

## Intarsia
As the cosies are made with several colours of yarn, the intarsia technique should be used to join them in. This involves using isolated strands or balls of yarn for each colour to avoid carrying them across the back of the work. You simply leave the unwanted colour hanging at the back of the work and pick up the required colour as you knit back and forth. Make sure you leave long enough strands to complete each area of colour. About 3 metres (10 feet) should be enough for the windows and door of the house.

Let's take an example: when you cast on you will need to use a strand of pink for one side of the house, a green strand for the door and then another strand of pink for the other side of the house. As you are knitting the house in garter stitch, when you come to change colour along

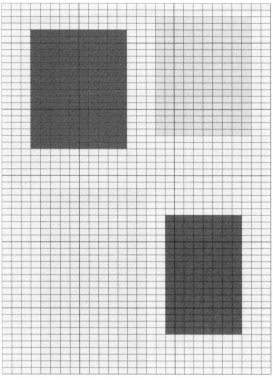

Tea cosy chart (each square represents 1 stitch)

a row, you will need to take the yarn for the colour you are about to knit with to the back of the work (between your needles) before knitting it. Once you have taken the strand to the back, you twist it around the yarn that you have just been working with so that there is no hole between the two colours; this should be done every time you change colour in any row.

When you have finished, the strands left hanging should be sewn in at the back of the work. To give both the inside and outside of the cosy a neat appearance, you should sew pink strands over the back of the pink knitting, green over green, and so on. This means that if your strands show at the front of the piece, you will hardly notice as they are the same colour as the knitting. It will also give the back of your work as neat a finish as you can get.

## FRONT AND BACK PIECES

Following the tea cosy chart, cast on 28sts in the following way:

Cast on 4sts in Yarn A, 11sts in Yarn B, 13sts with a separate strand of Yarn A. Follow the chart, working in G-st, until 56 rows are complete.

Break off Yarn A.

Continue in Yarn F for the rest of the piece.

## ROOF SHAPING

Using Yarn F, Knit 2 rows.
Next row: Purl.
Next row: Knit.
Next row: *K2tog, knit to last 2sts then k2tog.
Next row: Knit.*
Repeat from * to * until only 4sts remain.
Next row: K2tog twice.
Next row: K2tog.
Cast off.
The back is knitted in the same way, so repeat all of the above for the back piece.

## SIDES (MAKE 2)

*Using Yarn A, cast on 14sts.
Work in G-st for 52 rows.*
Leave the sts on a holder.
Repeat from * to * to make the second half of one of the sides.
Using Yarn A, with both sides on one needle (28sts all together), knit across all 28sts, thus joining them together. (This will become the opening for the spout on one side and the handle on the other.)
Knit 3 more rows.
Break off Yarn A.
Continue in Yarn F for the rest of the piece.

## ROOF SHAPING

Complete as for roof shaping the front.
Work other side of tea cosy in the same way.

## MAKING UP

Before putting the tea cosy together using backstitch and Yarn F, sew around the windows, dividing them into four using Yarn F. (Use the photo of the tea cosy as a guide.)

Place all sides of the tea cosy right side down on the ironing board (i.e. wrong side facing you), cover with a damp tea towel and press lightly with a hot iron.

Using Yarn A, sew up the sides of the tea cosy with the seams on the outside. Turn the cosy inside-out and overstitch the roof sections to it using Yarn F. Now sew the roof sections together, pinching them to make the roof stand tall.

Turn the cosy right side out and place over your teapot to work out how much you need to join the side pieces so that the spout and handle peek out. Remove from teapot and overstitch the two sides as necessary using Yarn A.

# KNITTED EGG COSY

## BACK
Using Yarn A, cast on 18sts and knit (G-st)
42 rows. Break off Yarn A. Using Yarn F, shape
the roof as follows.

## ROOF SHAPING
Next row: Knit.
Next row: Knit.
Next row: Purl.
Next row: Knit.
Next row: *K2tog, knit to the last 2sts, k2tog.
Next row: Knit*.
Repeat from * to * until you have 4sts left.
Next row: K2tog twice.
Next row: K2tog.
Fasten off.

## FRONT
Following the egg cosy chart, cast on 18sts in
the following way:

Cast on 2sts in Yarn A, cast on 7sts in Yarn B,
cast on 9sts in another strand of yarn A.

Follow the chart, working in G-st, until 42 rows
are complete.

## ROOF SHAPING
Complete the roof shaping as for the back.

## MAKING UP
Placing both sides of the egg cosy right side
down on the ironing board (i.e. wrong side facing
you), cover with a damp tea towel and lightly iron.

With the wrong sides together, use Yarn A to
sew up the seams on the outside. Using Yarn F
and overstitch, sew the outside of the roof
sections together.

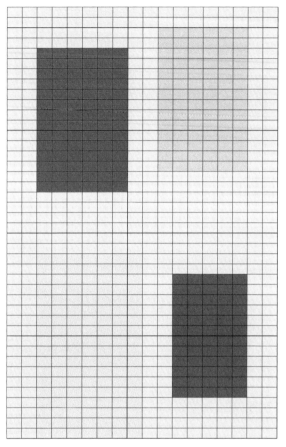

Egg cosy chart (each square represents 1 stitch)

# Best of the rest

There are some crafts that you just can't do from the comfort of your own home, usually because they involve specialist equipment, but please don't let that put you off. There are day courses available all over the country where you can learn a new skill, make something of your own, and generally soak up the environment and enthusiasm of a true artisan. The Directory on page 205 points you in the right direction for finding a course near you. Meanwhile, to give you an idea of what's involved and to help you choose what to do, here's a selection of some specialist crafts that I really enjoyed doing.

## BLACKSMITHING

Before I met Dean Agate, my experience of blacksmithing was limited to watching horses getting new shoes as a child. I hadn't been near a smithy for 15 years, and the moment Dean told me the hammer could spring back and knock my teeth out, I knew it wasn't something I'd be trying too often. But to make my own poker for the fireplace at Meadowgate and witness, first hand, Dean's undeniable skill and passion was worth the risk.

There are blacksmiths like Dean working independently in smithies across the UK today. Theirs is a life of hammering red hot metal and soldering irons, working from a furnace that burns at more than 1500 degrees Celsius at its core. So for anyone out there who likes to make a lot of noise and play with fire, this craft is just the ticket. There are day courses in blacksmithing where you can get an insight into the trade and, like me, have a go at making something of your own. Or why not buy a handmade item from your local blacksmith? A set of gates can cost from £160, and a poker like mine starts from about £30. It's handmade, one of a kind, and it'll last forever.

# GLASSBLOWING

Glassblowing is better than magic. It was the first craft I did for the TV series, and the first new craft I'd tried in years. At first, it was a bit like doing a bungee jump – I was fragile, glass is fragile, and really I couldn't have been more nervous. But after what must be the shortest apprenticeship in history – to professional glassblower Will Shakspeare – I managed to make the jump and transform a solid piece of glass into my very own tumbler (it still amazes me). It's up there as one my greatest achievements, and I had an over-whelming urge to pack in the day job and take up glassblowing full time. I've no doubt that whoever tries this craft will feel exactly the same as I did.

  The traditional process and tools used for glassblowing have changed little since Roman times. Glass used to be a luxury reserved only for the rich. The process for making it was also top secret, so much so that glassblowers in Venice were forbidden from leaving the city on pain of death. Thankfully, I made it out of Will's studio alive, and here's how I saw it happen, right before my eyes.

You take a solid piece of glass.
You heat it...
Blow it...
Stretch it...
Blow it again...
Heat it again...
Use one of Will's special tools and watch it start to take shape...
Take it off the metal rod and put it into the cooling cupboard to harden...
Simple!

This craft is clearly not one you can do at home, so if you want to create a pretty, prized possession of your own, you need to commit to at least a day course in a glassblowing studio or college. There are more than a hundred of these across the UK, many suitable for absolute beginners (see pages 207–8 and 211). Even if you don't have time for a course, it's still worth a visit to your local handmade glass shop – if just for a look at the amazing craftsmanship of artisans like Will.

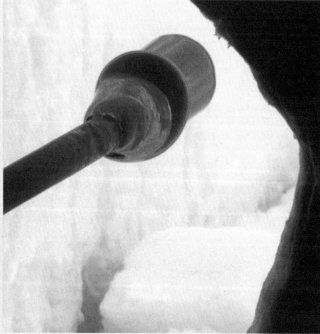

# POTTERY

There are plenty of pottery workshops where you can get your hands dirty, or you can try 'hobby' pottery from home, without a wheel – basically it's hand moulding of clay. You can then take it to your local pottery or ceramics shop to have it fired. You need to know which clay you're using in the first instance as different clays require different firing temperatures – for example, stoneware fires at a totally different temp from earthenware, and if they're fired incorrectly, there's a risk they'll melt or burst into flames!

Hand-moulding clay and painting ceramics are brilliant activities to do with kids. And if you get truly potty about this craft, you can actually buy your own mini kiln to use at home (see page 215).

I was lucky enough to get a lesson with Steve Harrison, who has a workshop in Middlesex. Steve makes truly beautiful pots, and with his help I even managed to make my own. It now has pride of place on the dresser at Meadowgate.

# SPINNING
# AND WEAVING

If knitting was like climbing Everest for me, learning how to turn the wool that gets sheared from my very own sheep into a ball of yarn that I could (potentially) knit with was, quite frankly, incredible. This craft takes real commitment and I know there won't be many of you running out to buy a traditional spinning-wheel. But if you fancy a one-day introduction to spinning, there are courses up and down the country (see page 218).

Hilary Charlesworth, who helped turn my wool into a beautiful handmade rug, runs a course in Hampshire that covers everything from preparing a fleece to spinning on a wheel. Prices for the course start from £40.

# STAINED GLASS

Britain has a centuries-old tradition of stained glass that can be seen in many of our churches and grand houses, but it was the Victorians who cast the net wide to include the rest of us when glaziers came up with ideas that allowed ordinary family homes to feature stained-glass window designs. Stained glass can have an absolutely glorious effect on an ordinary room, providing a welcome glow of colour on the dullest days, and truly uplifting shafts of coloured sunlight on brighter ones.

I met a stained-glass artist called Amanda Winfield, who helped me make a simple leaded light-catcher for the bathroom at Meadowgate. But more recently, I was able to take advantage of her incredible talent for restoring and recreating stained-glass windows from days of old. She designed a new front door window-pane for a Victorian house in Wolverhampton. It's absolutely beautiful.

If you want your own piece of stained glass in your home, expect to pay anything from £30 to £300 a square metre, depending on what colour or design you go for and whether the glass is machine-made or hand-blown. Or enrol on a day course and create something similar to my light-catcher (see pages 218–19).

# WILLOW-WORKING

The UK has a centuries-old tradition of willow-working, and basket-makers were once found in every village and town in the country – baskets have, in fact, been the ultimate shopper for thousands of years. But post 1950s, with the arrival of cheap cardboard and plastic, the willow-growing industry went into major decline and it was no longer worthwhile for farmers to grow it. Today it's mainly individual craftspeople working to keep the tradition alive. Devon-based weavers Richard and Sue Kerwood gave me an insight into their lives on the willow field and helped me make my own little basket, which I now use as an ornamental container in the kitchen at Meadowgate.

Handmade British baskets can be surprisingly inexpensive, and you can buy willow kits online to make things for your garden, such as fences, plant supports and fun things for the children. It's also a really accessible craft to get your kids involved with.

Turn to page 220 for information about how to find craftspeople and courses in your area.

# Search
# and find

# Sourcing old stuff

How do I convince everyone that auction rooms, antiques shops, reclamation yards, markets and the like are not scary places full of people who know more than you, and that they are not trying to rip you off? Well, I've spent the last ten years singing the praises of estate agents, so I suppose anything is possible!

There are numerous TV programmes and books that talk about money and antiques. This book is not one of them. I say buy what you want for the best price that you can negotiate and, unless it's a major investment (i.e. something you might need to sell one rainy day), don't worry about what it's worth. What's important is what it's worth to you. How much are you prepared to part with to have that item in your home?

In the decorative antiques world fashions change as much as they do on the catwalks. In my time I've seen trends for mahogany furniture, shell mirrors, spongeware pottery – oh, I could just go on and on and on. Such things soar and dip in price and, in some cases, soar again. I believe that these alterations in value aren't particularly relevant. It's actually about desire – how you feel when you look at something you hang on your wall or hold it in your hand. It's about what you see and what it does for your room.

Recently my other half came home with a vast print of a tiger standing against a mountain range. It was a style of painting that I really don't like, and when he showed it to me, this was written all over my face. I thought, 'Where on earth is he going to hang that?' How self-absorbed was I? It was for our three-year-old, who was absolutely *thrilled* with it.

I remember buying my first picture too. It was an embroidered garden scene bought from an antiques market in Hungerford. I loved it the way my son loves his tiger and mountain range, just because. Its value didn't matter to me then, so why should it matter to me now?

In the pages that follow I describe the main ways of sourcing old stuff for your home. The great thing about them all is that you never know what you're going to find. But don't think rummaging in such places is a quick fix. You need to invest real time and effort to find things you like that are worth buying.

# Choosing second-hand

Shopping for second-hand furniture and decorative things for the home is something I love doing, but it takes time and effort to get into the swing of it. My dad and my other half have taught me so much about always looking, looking, looking – looking at things and watching out for things you like. It's essentially being a shopaholic, but without a specific wishlist because your search is for what you might find that you can't live without, instead of searching for something that you think you need.

I look around the room in which I'm sitting and I can remember the occasion on which I received or bought every item. Nothing was just a matter of going to an out-of-town superstore, but that comes from years of practice. Even buying just one thing that you know you'll treasure is special. It's also highly addictive, so be warned!

I like walking out of the shop door with something that leaves with me and only me. Buying that one item in the shop is far better than purchasing one of 10,000 that many other people will have in their house. I also love buying things without price stickers (that doesn't mean they're priceless!) and it's a thrill to buy things for less than they're worth. I like buying things that other people can't love or no longer have any use for. I recently tried to buy two chairs for £140 that I know came from a skip somewhere. Someone had picked them up and was trying to sell them to me, but that's fine – it's knowing that something has travelled and has a history and personality I can relate to that makes me want it.

# Antiques shopping

The very name 'antiques shop' can be a bit frightening to the uninitiated, conjuring up images of fine furniture gleaming with the patina of centuries and having heart-stopping price tags attached. But, as you'll find if you dare to cross the threshold, these shops don't just sell 'antiques'. Most sell a whole bunch of stuff, some of which you'll find is just a few years old – it's basically a collection of second-hand things.

The two main problems that people have with antiques shops is (a) feeling that they could be caught out and charged a fortune for something worthless, or (b) fearing that they will be shown up for lacking knowledge. But look at it this way: no one walks into M&S thinking they can't buy knickers because they don't know how they're made. Of course they don't, and it doesn't matter one jot. What matters is that the shop is selling and the customer is interested in buying. It's the same with antiques shops and anywhere selling second-hand stuff. They need to sell it and you want to buy it. If you tell them what you can afford, they will answer you with a 'yes' or a 'no'. They are not out to get you. They want to sell to you. Remember, shops that don't trade fade! Everything is negotiable.

I visit antiques shops all the time, and my local one in Honiton has an amazing section devoted to second-hand linens. I can spend £5 or £100, and I'm always chuffed to bits to find something I like. Honestly, go down to your local antiques shop or market and have a look around. Even if you don't buy anything, it's a really fun thing to do.

**1** Don't be embarrassed to pop in and have a look around. Browsing is free and a great pastime. It's also a good way to build confidence and get used to this kind of shop.

**2** Positively *beam* at the shop assistant and forget everything you're told as a child about not touching. Remember, if you're buying something for your home, you have to like the feel of it, and that involves picking it up and holding it in your hands.

**3** Don't be afraid to ask questions, such as what type of wood it is, whether a picture is an original or a print, and how much things cost. So many items I look at in antiques shops don't have price tags. Often it's just a case of the owner not being able to keep up with the changing stock. It's not like going into a chain store where things are priced at source, or you have 25 of the same thing at one price. Antiques shops tend to be small, with few staff, and a constantly changing, individual stock.

**4** Don't make assumptions about what you see. If you're new to the game of antiques hunting, ask the prices of lots of different things so that you can start forming opinions about how much things cost.

**5** If you see something you really like but you want to do a bit of further research, take a photo, go online and find that thing. The Internet has revolutionised the world of antiques, and it favours the buyer.

**6** If you have an antique you've fallen out of love with and think might be worth something, you can always take it to your local antiques dealer and see if they'll swap it for something in their shop that you *do* want. If they love your old piece and you love their new piece, you're onto a winner.

**7** With a large item, such as a big table, some shops will let you take it home and try it out for size. Lots of things are sold on 'appro' (approval). You might need to pay a deposit, and you will almost certainly need to pay to get the item home (and back, if you don't like it after all), but it means you can try before you buy and that could be a great money-saver.

**8** Look for the odd ones out as these are usually the best bargains – for example, the single chair, or the piece of bronze in a display of silver. More likely than not, the dealer or seller will negotiate on the odd item in order to get it sold.

**9** Train your imagination to envisage an object in a new place. This is tough at first because it takes practice. Remember that it's what you like that counts. If it also happens to fit your home or purpose, so much the better.

**10** Most dealers are prepared to give a discount if asked nicely. It's usually about 10 per cent, but you can bargain a little harder if it relates to an unusual or especially large item that they might be glad to get rid of,

# Auctions

I am the daughter of an auctioneer, so I was lucky enough to be brought up surrounded by antiques, paintings and second-hand stuff my entire life. But although I go to auction houses week in, week out, I never, ever enter the bidding room. I can't. I'm just too competitive and I know that if someone else is after the thing I want, I will outbid them way more than I can afford. And that is bad! So if you're like me, do not enter the bidding room. Instead, try something known as commission bidding.

Commission bidding is when you go along to a pre-sale viewing and decide which items you'd like to bid on before the auction takes place. You put your maximum bid down there and then.

You start this process by picking up a catalogue from the front desk and this will tell you lot numbers and guide prices, and sometimes give you a brief description of the item. The guide price is the part to pay attention to as it gives you an indication of what the auctioneer is expecting for the item. Remember that you can bid a lower amount and take a gamble, but of course you run a greater risk of someone else outbidding you. It all depends what that item is worth to you.

Along with your catalogue, the front desk will also give you a form to complete if you want to bid on anything you see. Leave a figure that is the maximum you are prepared to spend. After that, it's basically down to the auctioneer, who will try to secure the items at the lowest price possible. He does this by bidding as low as the room or any other commission bid allows.

It is pot luck, but it pays to ask one of the auctioneers which items are selling for a lot of money and which are not. Just as in fashion, furniture and bits for the home go in and out of style too, so the auctioneer's advice could help you bid with a bit more confidence.

Sellers often put a 'reserve' or minimum sale price on their items before entering them into the sale. This is the minimum price they will accept, but that information is unlikely to be stated in the sale catalogue. A general rule of thumb is that the reserve price tends to be very slightly below the lowest end of the guide price.

One thing many people forget to take into account when buying at auctions is the 'buyer's premium'. This is basically a cost set by the auction house and added onto the total bid plus VAT. It can add quite a bit to the cost of an item, so beware. Buyer's premiums vary from auction house to auction house and it's worth checking what their percentage is before you start shopping.

If you end up bidding in the auction, know your limits. Don't let auction fever run away with you.

Auctions tend to take place throughout the week, which is a real nuisance for a lot of those who work full time. That's why commission bidding works for me. But if you've found something you passionately want and you're worried about losing it in the commission bid, you can attend through telephone bidding.

Furniture auctions are held all around the country, and each one will have its own house rules, so best ask at the desk before you go diving in. You should be able to get a copy of your local auction's calendar online (see page 205).

# Salvage and reclamation yards

There are rec yards and then there are rec yards. Some resemble smart outdoor warehouse shops and can be expensive. Others have things that look as though they have come straight from a rubbish tip, but essentially it's the same stuff without the tarting up.

While something that's covered in dust – or, in the case of rec yards, bird poo – can make you think you've found a bargain, that's not the point. Shopping at these places is *not* about bargain hunting. It's about spotting something you like and want, and envisaging what it could become and add to your home.

If you're going along for the first time, be prepared to use your imagination and see what you can make out of what's on offer. The selection of items available at salvage and rec yards is vast and varied. Often you'll find you like things that would have originally been used for a completely different purpose, or that have fallen out of fashion or into disrepair. If you can find a new and improved use for something, that's great. For example, most of the planters I used at Meadowgate were not originally used for plants: one was an old tin water trough, another was an old tin bath, and this dual purpose also happened with other stuff inside the house too. The old tin bath cost me a tenner and I planted it with a herb garden, aided and abetted by my friend Clemmie. It's lovely.

Rec yards and salvage yards are found all over the UK. Some call themselves architectural salvage yards, but you will find their prices, as with everything in the second-hand world, reflect the average income of the area and the desirability of such old and rusted things. In other words, don't expect to find any bargains in Bath.

In the fancier salvage yards you can pick up an old rusty fireplace and have them renovate it for you at a cost, or you can buy one that's already been renovated. In a place like Ray Cullop's, a salvage yard I go to in north London, there isn't so much hand-holding. I got the fire basket for the sitting room at Meadowgate for £50, but I had to renovate it myself. The elbow grease means the difference in price.

Try to visit the same places week after week in order to get to know the owner and let them get to know you, what you like and what you're after. This way, if you're after something specific, they'll look out for it.

# Markets

There are markets that sell furniture and second-hand things all over the country, but we seem to have forgotten about them, and many are at risk of closing down unless we rediscover them.

On as many Friday mornings as possible I go with my other half to Golborne Road in west London. It's a market and shopping street that's been there since the 1800s, but it became famous for its antiques in the 1950s. It sells tons of stuff – furniture, paintings, ceramics, chairs, benches – you name it and you'll find it. We've been going there for a long time, and the great thing is that the stall-holders have come to know us and what we like. Building up relationships with the people that run the stalls is essential. If you're nice to them, they'll remember you and what you like, and that's better than having an army of personal shoppers.

Never go shopping for anything in particular. Market shopping is like going on a nature walk and specifying what you want to see – that won't work because it's all a bit random. If you want to get your hands on the best stuff before everyone else, arrive as soon as the market opens, but if you're into bargaining hard for your finds, wait until the end of the day – stall-holders more often than not prefer sell stuff at a lower price than take it home.

Let me say straight away that browsing is not the way to find the gems in markets. You need to look thoroughly, dig deep and sift around right to the bottom of the pile – diamonds are smaller than bricks.

Markets have a no-returns policy, so when you're thinking of buying, look at your find, get a feel for it, and don't take it away until you're completely happy with what you're getting. If it's a seat, for example, make sure you sit on it before you buy. If it's a table, get the measuring tape out.

Finally, when you decide to buy, be prepared to barter and bargain, but don't expect things for free. Everyone needs to earn a living, so please remember to allow a bit of give and take.

# Skip-diving

There are no hard and fast rules for skip-diving. Actually, that's not technically true. There are rules, and they're called laws. You're not supposed to take anything out of a skip without first asking the owner's permission. OK, so ask the permission – that's easy. The hard bit is getting the confidence to walk up to a skip (or to the side of a road), have a rummage, and then have the guts to take something out if you want it.

One night we were two streets away from home after driving from Devon to London. Suddenly the car screeched to a halt and my other half leapt out and pulled a nearly new lawnmower from the side of the road. He tried to get it in between the car seats of our two boys, who were sound asleep in the back of the car, because it wouldn't fit on the roof – there was already a club fender up there that had travelled with us from Devon. (We rarely travel without 'finds': at the start of the weekend we'd driven down with a very large mirror on the roof. I used to be a keen listener to Radio 4, but this is no longer possible in the car because the clanging from the roof makes every other word inaudible.)

But back to the lawnmower – after a few sharp words from me, I convinced him to drop us at home before going back for it... and the bed that he'd spotted.

Skip-diving or skipping is one of the easiest things in the world to do. I have no advice or tips for it. All I'll say is that recycling, freecycling, all of that stuff that goes around and comes around, is a good thing. Why waste a perfectly good chair, or mirror, or bed, or lawnmower when it could be put to good use somewhere else?

(My other half lived in Hamburg when he was young and vividly recalls that on the last Thursday of every month people would put their unwanted wares out on the street for everyone to swap. They'd also put notes on things that were broken. Amazing! If only we did that here.)

Just one thing I would point out is that picking things out of skips or from the side of the road can be a little tricky if you have no means of transport. But there's no harm in knocking on a door and asking someone to keep the item for you until you can get back. Exchange it for a couple of beers. It's a great form of recycling, and it's also resourceful and thrifty.

# Internet

There's nothing I hate more than seeing something I want in a magazine and reading the words 'model's own'. Inevitably, this happens with interiors too, especially when old things and second-hand bits and pieces have been used. If you do see something you really like, in this book or anywhere else, get as many details about it as you can, then get online and search for it. The Internet has completely revolutionised the world of antiquing, recycling and buying second-hand. That look you want, or a pretty good approximation of it, *can* be achieved if you dedicate some time to research.

My favourite china pattern is Spode's Marlborough Sprays. Sadly, Spode no longer manufactures this design, but I'm still after a teapot and eventually I'll find one. The place I'm most likely to do that is on the Internet.

# Directory

This is a list of people and places mentioned in the book and featured in the TV series, plus others that I've found particularly useful. Where possible, it also includes information about where to find courses in each particular craft featured.

## ANTIQUES SHOPS & AUCTION CENTRES

*There's no way I can give a list of antiques shops around the country, so below you will find just a few of my favourites, where I found loads of stuff for Meadowgate.*

*As for auctions, they take place everywhere. To find those near you I recommend signing up to Antiques Gazette (www.antiquestradegazette. com), which has a massive calendar of auctions and antiques markets, or logging onto any of the Auction Finder sites listed below.*

### Auction Finder
www.auctionhammer.co.uk
www.ebay.co.uk
www.ukauctioneers.com
www.ukwebstart.com
*Visit any of these websites to find an auction near you.*

### Fagin's Antiques
The Old Whiteways Cider Factory
Hele
Exeter
Devon EX5 4PW
Tel: 01392 882062
www.faginsantiques.com

### Fountain Antique Centre
132 High Street
Honiton
Devon EX14 1JP
Tel: 01404 42074

### Honiton Antique Centre
Abingdon House
136 High Street
Honiton
Devon EX14 1JP
Tel: 01404 42108
www.abingdonhouseantiques.co.uk

### The Lacquer Chest
75 Kensington Church Street
London W8 4BG
Tel: 020 7937 1306
www.lacquerchest.com

### Lawrence's Auction House
The Linen Yard
South Street
Crewkerne
Somerset TA18 8AB
Tel: 01460 73041
www.lawrences.co.uk

### Les Couilles du Chien
65 Golborne Road
London W10 5NP
Tel: 020 8968 0099
www.lescouillesduchien.co.uk

### Lost Property Auctions
www.governmentauctionsuk.com
*Also known as 'airport auctions', these are held by public bodies, e.g. airports, railways, the police and Post Office, to sell unclaimed or undeliverable items. They are often organised by the auction house that provides the best tender for the work, so might not take place close to where the lost property originates.*

### UK Auctioneers
4 Shipgate Street
Chester
Cheshire CH1 1RT
Tel: 01244 345933
www.ukauctioneers.com
*Browse auction catalogues online, leave commission bids, check auction sale results and much more.*

## BLACKSMITHING

*I had so much fun learning the basics of blacksmithing, and even managed to make something really useful. I really recommend you try it.*

### Dean Aggett
Meadow Forge
Hillside Barn
Cadeleigh
Nr Exeter
Devon EX16 8RZ
Tel: 01884 855888 or 07773 006743
www.meadowforge.co.uk
*Dean showed me how to make my own poker. He offers courses in his workshop, but there are blacksmiths all over the country offering courses near you.*

### National School of Blacksmithing
www.hct.ac.uk
Tel: 0800 032 1986
*Part of Herefordshire College of Technology; offers a range of courses.*

### Worshipful Company of Blacksmiths
www.blacksmithscompany.org.uk
*The website has information about courses all around the country.*

## CAKE DECORATING

*To find a course or workshop near you, see below or log onto some of the websites listed under Craft Courses.*

### Little Venice Cake Company (Mich Turner)
15 Manchester Mews
London W1U 2DX
Tel: 020 7486 5252
www.lvcc.co.uk
*Mich Turner's company runs master classes in cake decorating, and Mich herself taught me the basics of icing and making sugarpaste roses. From January 2011 her own range of equipment can be found in all good cake-decorating stores, as well as at John Lewis, Hobbycraft and The Range (see page 208).*

### Squires Kitchen
3 Waverley Lane
Farnham
Surrey GU9 8BB
Tel: 0845 225 5671 or 5672
www.squires-shop.com
*Recommended by Mich Turner (see previous entry), this shop, and its website, offers a huge range of cake-making equipment.*

## CANDLE-MAKING

*There are candle-making courses available all around the UK. To find one near you, see below or log onto some of the websites listed under Craft Courses.*

### British Candle-makers Federation
Tel: 020 7248 4726
www.britishcandlemakers.org
*This organisation represents candle-makers and their suppliers, but offers lots of useful safety information on its website.*

### David Constable
28 Blythe Road
London W14 0HA
Tel: 020 7602 4031
www.candlemakers.co.uk
*Apart from making wonderful candles, David also runs candle-making courses. He taught me how to make teacup candles.*

## CHILDREN'S FURNISHINGS

*Again, it's impossible to give a comprehensive list of shops and websites specialising in things for children. Here are a few I like, but there are loads more to choose from if you do an online search.*

### Great Little Trading Company
PO Box 336
Birkenhead CH25 9DN
Tel: 0151 514 1340
www.gltc.co.uk
*Mail order and online company offering something for virtually every need connected with children.*

**KidzDens Ltd**
Unit 11E
Elsecar Heritage Centre
Wath Road
Elsecar
Barnsley S74 8HJ
Tel: 01226 749729
www.kidsdens.co.uk
*Sells a lovely range of children's furniture and accessories.*

**Win Green Trading Company**
The Bothy
Clock House
Heath Road
Coxheath
Kent ME17 4PG
Tel: 01622 746516
www.wingreen.co.uk
*An unusual toy company specialising in themed play dens and accessories. The riding stable, sheriff's office and boathouse are a joy.*

## CONSERVATION & RESTORATION

*Conservation is a way of preserving our cultural heritage for our children in the future. Restoration is the skill of giving broken-down things a new lease of life. If you own, buy or have a love of old things that you want to hand down through generations, the following websites could come in useful.*

**British Association of Antique Furniture Restorers**
Tel: 01305 854822
www.bafra.org.uk
*Founded in 1979 for those who love, conserve and restore antique furniture.*

**Institute of Conservation**
Tel: 020 7785 380
www.icon.org.uk
*A great site for anyone interested in the conservation and preservation of our cultural heritage. Its Conservation Register tells you how to care for art and antiques, and how to find a local conservator. The site also offers information about careers and training in this field.*

## COOKERS

*Love them or loathe them, no one can deny that Agas are iconic. They might cost a lot, but if treated well, will probably last forever. You can make a saving if you buy a reconditioned model – just do an online search to find a supplier in your area.*

**Aga**
Juno Drive
Leamington Spa
Warwickshire CV31 3RG
Tel: 0845 712 5207
www.agafoodservice.com

## CRAFT COURSES & MATERIALS

*Colleges, workshops and individuals all around the UK offer courses in a huge variety of subjects, and it's impossible to give a detailed listing here. The following sources can provide the information you need to find a course, or offer online courses that are accessible no matter where you live.*

**Art Courses**
www.artcourses.co.uk
*A useful site that allows you to search by subject and area for the ideal course near you.*

**Craft Fair**
www.craft-fair.co.uk
*Offers a wide range of craft courses around the UK, plus a few overseas.*

**Craft Links**
www.craftlinks.co.uk
*A website offering lists of craft-makers and suppliers, plus course information around the country.*

**Craft Search**
www.craft-search.co.uk
*Although predominantly a listing of craft suppliers, this site does have some information about craft courses, workshops and holidays.*

**Designer Courses**
Tel: 08456 809362
www.designercourses.co.uk
*Here you can find short, London-based courses in various crafts, the selection varying from term to term. At the time of writing those on offer include leatherwork, hat-making and textile art.*

**Fiskars**
Tel: 01480 896866
www.fiskarscraft.co.uk
*Fiskars are renowned for their scissors; I've got wonderful left-handed ones. But there's a lot more to this crafty company, and the website is well worth a look.*

**Floodlight**
http://london.floodlight.co.uk
*Lists all courses on offer throughout the UK.*

**Hobbycraft**
www.hobbycraft.co.uk
Tel: 01202 596100
*The UK's leading out-of-town art and craft retailer, Hobbycraft caters for more than 250 different activities. It also offers online projects for various levels of ability.*

**Hot Courses**
www.hotcourses.com
*This site makes it really easy to find the right course and location for you.*

**The Range**
www.therange.co.uk
*A chain of stores offering a wide selection of art and craft materials, soft furnishings, lighting, homewares and much more.*

**Space2create**
www.space2create.net
*City & Guilds centre offering a range of online supported craft courses.*

**Workers' Educational Association**
Tel: 020 7426 3450
www.wea.org.uk
*A voluntary adult education movement that offers courses across the country.*

**CRAFT FAIRS**
*It seems that not a weekend goes by without a craft fair taking place somewhere in the UK. You can find lists of them on the sites below.*

**Craft Fair**
www.craft-fair.co.uk

**Craft Links**
www.craftlinks.co.uk

## CROCHET
*There are crochet courses available all around the UK. To find one near you, see below or log onto some of the websites listed under Craft Courses.*

**Floodlight**
http://london.floodlight.co.uk
*Lists all courses on offer all around the UK.*

**Erika Knight**
PO Box 1253
Berkhamsted
Hertfordshire HP4 1WG
Tel: 07791 151159
www.erikaknight.co.uk
*Erika, who taught me to crochet, is a renowned knitwear designer and respected consultant to the fashion and yarn industry. She is the author of numerous knitting and crochet books and has lectured at the Victoria & Albert Museum in London, as well as at leading art institutions and universities. You can contact her if you would like to plan a workshop or an event, or possibly an evening get-together, knit in or knit out!*

**Knitting & Crochet Guild**
www.knitting-and-crochet-guild.org.uk
*The guild offers help, advice and friendship to anyone interested in knitting and crochet. It also runs courses and workshops.*

**Learn to Crochet**
www.emagister.co.uk
*A selective listing of crochet courses around the UK.*

**Ravelry**
www.ravelry.com
*An online knit and crochet community that has lots of lovely free patterns and information about yarns and much more.*

**UK Hand Knitting Association**
www.bhkc.co.uk
*An alphabetical listing by county of both knitting and crochet courses all around the UK and Northern Ireland.*

## CURTAINS
*Well-made curtains can cost a lot, so it's worth seeing if you can get them second-hand. Try the source below, or do an online search: you might find the perfect fit on eBay.*

**The Curtain Exchange**
www.thecurtainexchange.net
*A nationwide chain of shops that sells both new and second-hand curtains.*

**Curtain Suppliers**
www.curtainsuppliers.com
*An easy-to-use site that helps you to find local curtain suppliers, and also provides useful information about measuring up.*

## FABRICS
*The following companies all sell lovely fabrics, some of them more unusual than others. Check out the designs on their websites.*

**Vanessa Arbuthnott Fabrics**
The Tallet
Calmsden
Nr Cirencester
Gloucestershire GL7 5ET
Tel: 01285 831437
www.vanessaarbuthnott.co.uk
*Vanessa owns one of the inspirational homes featured in the TV series. She designs the lovely fabrics she uses, and her collections complement each other by sharing colours and including*

*useful coordinates, such as checks, stripes, spots and florals.*

**Laura Ashley Home Interiors**
Tel: 0871 983 5999
www.lauraashley.com
*A familiar name that offers attractive and affordable fabrics.*

**Busby & Busby**
The Old Stables
Winterborne White Church
Blandford Forum
Dorset DT11 9AW
Tel: 01258 221211
www.busbyfabric.com
*This company supplied a lot of the fabric used at Meadowgate.*

**Chelsea Textiles**
13 Walton Street
London SW3 2HX
Tel: 020 7584 5544
www.chelseatextiles.com
*Renowned for its collection of hand-embroidered fabrics, many of which recreate antique designs.*

**Colefax & Fowler**
110 Fulham Road
London SW3 6HU
Tel: 020 7244 7427
www.colefax.com
*Offers elegant and subtle designs that reflect the classic English style.*

**de Le Cuoña**
150 Walton Street
London SW3 2JJ
Tel: 020 702 0800
www.delecuona.co.uk
*Innovative and luxurious fabrics made in linen, silk, bamboo and jute, many in interesting weaves.*

**Hansons Fabrics**
Station Road
Sturminster Newton
Dorset DT10 1BD
Tel: 01258 472698
www.hansonsfabrics.co.uk

*Sells high-quality fabrics, plus a host of haberdashery and craft materials. This shop also sells sewing machines, and it's where I got mine.*

### The Isle Mill
Tower House
Ruthvenfield Road
Inveralmond
Perth PH1 3UN
Tel: 01738 609090
www.islemill.com
*A long-established Scottish company that designs and weaves distinctive fabrics in natural fibres. Many take their inspiration from the colours of the Highlands. The company also undertakes design projects to meet clients' specific requirements.*

### Lewis & Wood
Woodchester Mill
North Woodchester
Stroud
Gloucestershire GL5 5NN
Tel: 01453 878517
www.lewisandwood.co.uk
*Here's something different... big prints on natural fabrics, witty wallpaper designs, and also wide-width wallpapers.*

### Malabar
31–33 South Bank Business Centre
Ponton Road
London W8 5BL
Tel: 020 7501 4200
www.malabar.co.uk
*This company sells handloom fabrics in vibrant colours and textures, all produced by weaving cooperatives in Kerala, southwest India. It also sells a wide range of paint colours designed to work with the fabric collections.*

### Romo Fabrics
Lowmoor Road
Kirkby-in-Ashfield
Nottingham NG17 7DE
Tel: 01623 756699
www.romofabrics.com
*A long-established family company that designs exclusive fabrics and wall coverings in classic and contemporary prints.*

### Volga Linen
Unit 1, Eastlands Industrial Estate
Leiston
Suffolk IP16 4LL
Tel: 0844 499 1609
www.volgalinen.co.uk
*Although best known for its beautiful linens from Russia and Europe, this company also sells fabrics in classic designs and ready-to-hang curtains.*

## FIREPLACES
*You can buy fireplace inserts, surrounds, fire baskets and all sorts of related hardware at reclamation yards and antique warehouses all over the country. You can choose to buy a fireplace already restored, or you can roll up your sleeves and do the dirty work yourself. Ask the advice of the sellers, and definitely look online to find out about restoring and fitting fireplaces. It can be quite an expensive business when you add up the costs of buying, fitting and getting them working again, but they're worth it when you consider the impact they make on a room.*

## FLOWER ARRANGING
*If you love flowers, as I do, it's worth learning how to do them justice in your arrangements. To find a course or workshop near you, see below or log onto some of the websites listed under Craft Courses.*

### Judith Blacklock School of Floristry
4/5 Kinnerton Place South
London SW1X 8FH
Tel: 020 7235 6235
www.judithblacklock.com
*Judith gave me the fantastic tips that are included in this book. She also offers courses in flower arranging and floral design, as well as in flower painting and botanical art.*

### British Florist Association
Tel: 0844 8007299
www.britishfloristassociation.org
*For those who want to pursue flower arranging professionally, the society has a useful training and qualifications link.*

**National Association of Flower Arrangement Societies**
Tel: 020 7247 5567
www.nafas.org.uk
*Lists local flower-arranging groups where you can learn floristry.*

**Royal Horticultural Society**
Tel: 0845 260 5000
www.rhs.org.uk
*Dedicated to promoting good gardening, the RHS has an online advice service, offering tips about growing your own fruit and veg, and providing answers to your plant problems.*

## GARDEN

*It's easy to find plants, pots and garden furniture in nurseries and superstores, but sometimes you want something a bit different – something that will set your garden apart. The individuals and companies listed below can help you achieve just that.*

**Candace Bahouth**
*Candace is an artist who works in a variety of media and makes beautiful objects, including garden ornaments. See page 214 for her details.*

**Baileys Home & Garden**
Whitecross Farm
Bridstow
Hereford HR9 6JU
Tel: 01989 561931
www.baileyshomeandgarden.com
*Mark and Sally Bailey offer lots of recycled furniture ideas for truly unique interiors, plus fantastic ideas for lighting.*

**Clemmie Hambro**
Tel: 01777 0594303
www.clemmiehambro.com
*Clemmie qualified in horticulture at the English Gardening School, and designed the garden at Meadowgate.*

**Petersham Nurseries**
Off Petersham Road
Richmond
Surrey TW10 7AG
Tel: 020 8940 5230
www.petershamnurseries.com
*We visited Petersham for the TV series because, apart from selling plants, it's a great place for ideas on how to get that sunny lunch feel, indoors and outdoors, every day in your home. The café and restaurant are also worth a visit.*

## GILDING GLASS

*To find a course or workshop near you, see below or log onto some of the websites listed under Craft Courses.*

**London Gilding (Christine McInnes)**
110 Gloucester Ave
London NW1 8JA
Tel: 07947 013532
londongilding@gmail.com
*Christine McInnes introduced me to reverse painting and the craft of gilding glass. She also runs workshops.*

## GLASSBLOWING

*I still find it astonishing that I managed to make a perfectly usable blue glass. It's one of the most satisfying things I've ever done. For further information about glassblowing and courses, see below and the listings under Stained Glass.*

**Shakspeare Glass (Will Shakspeare)**
Riverside Place
Taunton
Somerset TA1 1JJ
Tel: 01823 333422 or 07977 000962
www.shakspeareglass.co.uk
*Will Shakspeare produces fantastic handmade glass and also runs courses. He helped me to make my blue glass, and made several more to provide a complete set for Meadowgate.*

## INSPIRATION & INFORMATION

*During the course of the TV series, we visited many inspirational places. They certainly gave me great ideas, and I'm sure they will for you too. There are also lots of publications to plunder for ideas, some of which are listed below. Remember too that old books about interiors can be just as useful as new ones.*

## Inspirational designers

### Kaffe Fassett

www.kaffefassett.com
*Kaffe is a wonderful designer who works in a variety of media. He's well known for his colourful knitwear and tapestries, but he's also a huge fan of mosaic. His multicoloured porch certainly inspired me.*

### Anouska Hempel Design

27 Adam & Eve Mews
London W8 6UG
Tel: 020 7938 151
www.anouskahempeldesign.com
*Anouska is an incredible designer, renowned for her unique and luxurious style, which, she assures me, can be replicated for not a lot of money.*

### Cath Kidston

2nd Floor, Frestonia
Freston Road
London W10 6TH
Tel: 020 7313 8398
www.cathkidston.co.uk
*We showed some of Cath's distinctive designs and styling in the TV series. She sells a lovely range of kitsch flowery accessories and fabrics for the home.*

## Inspirational ideas

### Not on the High Street

T22 Tideway Yard
125 Mortlake High Street
London SW14 8SN
Tel: 0845 259 1359
www.notonthehighstreet.com
*Dedicated to offering stylish and unusual items that come direct from creative small businesses.*

## Inspirational places

### Burgh Island Hotel

Bigbury-on-Sea
South Devon TQ7 4BG
Tel: 01548 810514
www.burghisland.com
*This wonderful art deco hotel, built in 1929, stands on its own island and is an absolute gem. Its style definitely influenced the yellow bathroom at Meadowgate.*

### Lanhydrock House

Lanhydrock
Bodmin
Cornwall PL30 5AD
Tel: 01208 265950
www.nationaltrust.org.uk
*Although this splendid house dates from the 17th century, it is now largely Victorian thanks to refurbishing after a fire in 1881. It is the last word in 19th-century luxury and modernity, and its scale and design are still awe-inspiring.*

### Maunsel House

North Newton
North Petherton
Bridgwater
Somerset TA7 0BU
Tel: 01278 661076
www.maunselhouse.co.uk
*While it is basically a magnificent 13th-century manor, Maunsel House has parts dating back to 1066 and others that show the hand of later periods. From its huge stone fireplaces to its oak panelling, old master paintings, Regency french windows and Victorian sporting trophies, it has a wealth of features that would inspire the most hard-hearted modernist.*

### Port Eliot

St Germans
Saltash
Cornwall PL12 5ND
Tel: 01503 230211
www.porteliot.co.uk
*Originally a priory dating from 937, Port Eliot has been extended several times since then. I love its faded curtains and threadbare rugs, its burnished*

furniture and wonderful paintings. It's a real family home, even if the kitchen is 100 metres from the dining room! There are tons of ideas I'd like to plunder, and one day I will...

## Inspirational publications

### All About You
www.allaboutyou.com
*This site brings together a wealth of information from six of the UK's best-loved magazines:* She, Good Housekeeping, Coast, Country Living, Prima *and* House Beautiful. *If you're in need of inspiration, just look at its Homes section, which is full of ideas for decorating and furnishing.*

### Antiques Collectors Club
www.antiquecollectorsclub.com
*Publishes a wide variety of books on decorative art and antiques, gardening and architecture, fashion and design, art and photography.*

### Homes & Gardens
www.homesandgardens.com
*Inspirational homes, gardens, shopping and decorating ideas from* Homes & Gardens *magazine.*

### The House Directory
PO Box 300
London W11 3WE
Tel: 020 7221 6600
www.thehousedirectory.com
*A fantastic sourcebook for interior and garden decoration.*

### Period Ideas
www.periodideas.com
*If you're renovating your home, this online resource from* Period Ideas *magazine will prove invaluable.*

## KNITTING
*There's been a great revival of interest in knitting over the last few years, and there are loads of courses available that will teach you how (see below or log onto some of the websites listed under Craft Courses).*

### Knitting & Crochet Guild
www.knitting-and-crochet-guild.org.uk
*The guild offers help, advice and friendship to anyone interested in knitting and crochet. It also runs courses and workshops.*

### Ravelry
www.ravelry.com
*An online knit and crochet community that has lots of lovely free patterns and information about yarns and much more.*

### Rowan Wool
Tel: 01484 681881
www.knitrowan.com
*An online company that produces high-quality yarns and publishes a twice-yearly magazine of handknit designs from acclaimed designers.*

### UK Hand Knitting Association
www.bhkc.co.uk
*An alphabetical listing by county of both knitting and crochet courses all around the UK and Northern Ireland.*

### The Wool Sanctuary (Suzie Johnson)
12 Trevelyan Road
Weston-super-Mare
Somerset BS23 3BH
Tel: 01934 414906 or 07812 365017
www.thewoolsanctuary.com
*Suzie, who owns the Wool Sanctuary, succeeded where my grandmother failed – she taught me how to knit. Her lovely shop stocks yarn and knitting kits. She also runs workshops and a knit school, gives private tuition, and has founded a successful knit club.*

## LAMPSHADES & LIGHTING

*Lighting can make or break a room, so it's well worth getting the right fittings, bulbs and shades.*

### Baileys Home & Garden
*See Garden section for details of this company.*

### Hot Courses
www.hotcourses.com
*Search on this site for lampshade-making courses or workshops.*

### Shades of Choice  (Eileen Garsed)
Tel: 01275 373025
www.shadesofchoice.talktalk.net
*Eileen helped me to make a bespoke lampshade. You can commission her to make your own exclusive shade, or buy the special equipment from her that you need to make own shades.*

### Vaughan Designs
G1, Chelsea Harbour Design Centre
Lots Road
London SW10 0XE
Tel: 020 7349 4600
www.vaughandesigns.com
*Produces a range of stylish and classical lighting.*

## MATTRESS SUPPLIERS

*For a good night's sleep you need a good mattress, and the following companies can supply just that.*

### Natural Mat
99 Talbot Road
London W11 2AT
Tel: 020 7985 0474
www.naturalmat.co.uk
*This company makes hand-crafted baby mattresses that are breathable, washable and non-allergenic.  They are also a good source for odd-sized mattresses.*

### Vi-Spring Ltd
Ernesettle Lane
Ernesettle
Plymouth PL5 2TT
Tel: 01752 366311

www.vispring.co.uk
*Every Vi-Spring mattress is handmade from natural, breathable materials.*

## MOSAIC

*I'm a convert to the charms of mosaic, and I really recommend you find a course so that you can be converted too (see below or log onto some of the websites listed under Craft Courses).*

### Candace Bahouth
Tel: 01749 890433 or 07930 894194
www.mosaicbahouth.com
*Candace is an artist who produces the most amazing work, including mosaic garden ornaments and furniture. In fact, her stunning objects inspired me to introduce more colour to Meadowgate's garden.*

### Emma Biggs
Tel: 020 7272 2603 or 07971 812437
www.emmabiggsmosaic.net
www.mymosaicworkshop.co.uk
*Emma helped me to make my mosaic table. She runs courses, and her Mosaic Workshop sells mosaic materials and tools. An exhibition of her work can be seen on www.yorkstmarys.org.uk*

### British Association for Modern Mosaics
www.bamm.org.uk
*This organisation promotes the understanding and appreciation of mosaic through exhibitions and workshops.*

## PAINTS

*Paint is paint, right? Wrong! There's a huge variety to choose from, and different manufacturers really do produce noticeably different types. I especially like the so-called 'heritage paints' because the colours are unique and have a lovely chalky finish.*

### Farrow & Ball
Uddens Estate
Wimborne
Dorset BH21 7NL

Tel: 01202 876141
www.farrow-ball.com
*The beauty of Farrow & Ball paints is that they have the most amazing selection of colours. They're unique and beautiful, and they last.*

### Nutshell Natural Paints
Unit 3, Leigham Units
Silverton Road
Matford Park
Exeter
Devon EX2 8HY
Tel: 01392 823760
www.nutshellpaints.com
*As they're eco-friendly and made from natural raw materials, Nutshell paints are particularly good in children's rooms.*

## POTTERY
*Throwing pots seems to me like a sophisticated form of making mud pies – you get agreeably messy, but produce something lasting and useful at the end of it. If you want to learn pottery, see below, or log onto some of the sites in the Craft Courses section.*

### Bath Potters' Supplies
Unit 18
Fourth Avenue
Westfield Trading Estate
Radstock
Nr Bath BA3 4XE
Tel: 01761 411077
www.bathpotters.co.uk
*On this site you can get everything you need to make your own pottery, including mini kilns.*

### Brixton Pottery Ltd
9 Harpers Lane
Presteigne
Powys LD8 2AN
Tel: 01544 260577
www.brixtonpottery.com
*This small company produces very pretty spongeware pottery, which I love. There are several pieces on the dresser at Meadowgate.*

### Craft Potters Association
25 Foubert's Place
London W1F 7QF
Tel: 020 7439 3377
www.cpaceramics.co.uk
*This is the national body representing ceramic artists in the UK. It has links to other organisations offering courses around the country.*

### Steve Harrison
40 Brodie Road
Enfield
Middlesex EN2 0ET
Tel: 020 8482 4169
www.steveharrison.co.uk
*Steve, who makes salt-glazed ware and a wide variety of architectural items, reintroduced me to the joy of throwing pots. He lectures part-time at Camberwell College of Art and is also involved with practical workshops that include building kilns and related equipment.*

### Nicholas Mosse Pottery
Bennettsbridge
Co. Kilkenny
Ireland
Tel: 353 (0)56 772 7505
www.nicholasmosse.com
*Nicholas makes beautiful pottery – clean, simple shapes decorated in the style of traditional Irish spongeware. I love it.*

### Potteries Museum
Uttoxeter Road
Longton
Stoke-on-Trent
Derbyshire ST3 1PQ
Tel: 01782 237777
www.stokemuseums.org.uk
*This is one of several museums that traces the history of the pottery industry. It offers workshops and a changing programme of exhibitions.*

### Studio Pottery
PO Box 634
Haywards Heath
Sussex RH16 1WT
www.studiopottery.co.uk
*This site acts as a gallery for a variety of potters,*

and their stunning work is all for sale. It also has a directory of potters who run courses.

**Valentine Clays Ltd**
The Sliphouse
18–20 Chell St
Hanley
Stoke-on-Trent
Derbyshire ST1 6BA
Tel: 01782 271200
www.valentineclays.co.uk
*Recommended by potter Steve Harrison, this company is a good source of clay and other materials for making pottery.*

## QUILTING
*If you don't have the time or inclination to make your own quilt, you can buy one online or in antiques shops/warehouses that sell old linen.*

**Jo Cowill**
Cowslip Workshops
Newhouse Farm
St Stephens
Launceston
Cornwall PL15 8JX
Tel: 01566 772654
www.cowslipworkshops.co.uk
*Jo helped me to make a fantastic quilt for one of my children. She runs a range of classes, and also sells a wide variety of fabrics and quilting supplies.*

**Jen Jones Welsh Quilts**
Pontbrendu
Llanybydder
Ceredigion SA40 9UJ
Tel: 01570 480610
www.jen-jones.com
*I absolutely love Jen's website. It sells a fabulous collection of quilts, both vintage and new. Jen also offers a range of quilting workshops and courses.*

**Quilters Guild of the British Isles**
Tel: 01904 613242
www.quiltersguild.org.uk
*This site offers tips and techniques, and also lists quilting teachers all around the country.*

## RUGS
*I prefer rugs to fitted carpets – they just seem cosier. If you fancy making your own rag rug, see below, or log onto some of the websites listed under Craft Courses.*

**Fenland Sheepskin Company**
Axe Road
Colley Lane Industrial Estate
Bridgwater
Somerset TA6 5LN
Tel: 01278 427586
www.fenland-sheepskin.co.uk
*This company supplied the sheepskin rugs for Meadowgate, and very cosy they are too.*

**Debbie Siniska**
Tel: 01580 201015
www.debbiesiniska.co.uk
*Debbie is a textile artist who taught me how to make a zingy rag rug. Her website lists workshops and courses in rugging, felt-making and bead-work, and also sells a range of rug-making tools. Her latest book,* Rag Rugs: Old into New, *is available through her website.*

## SALVAGE & RECLAMATION YARDS
*Like antiques shops and warehouses, there are salvage and reclamation yards all over the place. Below are some of my favourites. Search online at Salvoweb (see opposite) for your local yards.*

**Bygones Architectural Reclamation Ltd**
Nackington Road
Canterbury
Kent CT4 7BA
Tel: 0800 0433 012
www.bygones.net
*One of the largest reclamation yards in the UK, Bygones provides high-quality architectural antiques. You can view their stock online.*

**Cheshire Demolition & Excavation Contractors**
72 Moss Lane
Macclesfield
Cheshire SK11 7TT
Tel: 01625 424433

www.cheshiredemolition.co.uk
*Don't let the name deceive you – this company also specialises in reclamation, supplying architectural antiques, reclaimed building materials and traditional fireplaces.*

**Cox's Architectural Salvage Yard**
10 Fosseway Business Park
Moreton-in-Marsh
Gloucestershire GL56 9NQ
Tel: 01608 652505
www.coxsarchitectural.co.uk
*Offers a large and varied stock of reclaimed building materials and architectural antiques.*

**Lassco**
30 Wandsworth Road
London SW8 2LG
Tel: 020 7394 2100
www.lassco.co.uk
*A gloriously mismatched collection of pieces, all housed in a disused church.*

**Park Royal Salvage**
Lower Place Wharf
Acton Lane
London NW10 7AB
Tel: 020 8961 3627
www.parkroyalsalvage.co.uk
*Ray Cullop runs this salvage yard and has sold me some great stuff over the years.*

**Retrouvius Reclamation and Design**
2A Ravensworth Road
London NW10 5NR
Tel: 020 8960 6060
www.retrouvius.com
*Offers an ever-changing selection of architectural salvage, and keeps a good stock of hardwood worktops.*

**Salvoweb**
www.salvoweb.com
*Visit this site to find your nearest salvage or reclamation yard.*

**Viking Reclamation**
Cow House Lane
Armthorpe Industrial Estate
Armthorpe, Doncaster
South Yorkshire DN3 3EE
Tel: 01302 835449
www.reclaimed.co.uk
*Sells reclaimed building materials, oak flooring, and a wide range of architectural salvage, all viewable online.*

## SCREEN-PRINTING
*Although it requires some special equipment, screen-printing is surprisingly straightforward. To find a course near you, see below or log onto some of the websites listed under Craft Courses.*

**Cadisch**
Unit 1, Finchley Industrial Estate
879 High Road
London N12 8QA
Tel: 020 9492 0444
www.cadisch.com
*This company sells a wide range of screen-printing products.*

**Double Elephant Print Workshop**
Exeter Phoenix
Bradninch Place
Gandy Street
Exeter
Devon EX4 3LS
Tel: 07855 206659
www.doubleelephant.org.uk
*This workshop offers a range of courses in print-making. It's also where I got expert help from Emma Molony (see below).*

**Emma Molony**
Tel: 07855 512753
www.emmamolony.com
*Emma taught me how to screen-print and helped me to make some fantastic wallpaper for my downstairs loo. The design can be bought online from her website.*

**Selectasine**
Old Portsmouth Road
Peasmarsh
Guildford
Surrey GU3 1LZ

Tel: 01483 565800
www.selectasine.com
*Recommended by screen-printer Emma Molony, this company sells a wide range of screen-printing products.*

## SOAP-MAKING
*Making soap feels like alchemy – lots of fizzing, steaming and stirring, followed by a magical end result. To find a workshop near you, log onto some of the websites listed under Craft Courses.*

### Odds and Suds  (Jenny Elesmore)
20 North Street
Ashburton
Devon TQ13 7QD
Tel: 01364 654882

30 Pannier Market Shops
Tavistock
Devon PL19 0AL
Tel: 01822 618111
www.oddsandsuds.com
*Jenny Elesmore makes wonderful soap and bath bombs. She taught me how to make my own soap, and will teach you too if you sign up for one of her workshops.*

## SPINNING & WEAVING
*To find a course or workshop near you, see below and also log onto some of the websites listed under Craft Courses.*

### Fibrecrafts
Tel: 01483 565800
www.fibrecrafts.com
*This online company sells a wide range of craft materials, including fibres, yarns, fabrics and dyes.*

### Handweavers Studio & Gallery
140 Seven Sisters Road
London N7 7NS
Tel: 020 7272 1891
www.handweavers.co.uk

*Sells an extensive range of materials and equipment for the whole world of fibre art and textile crafts. Also offers numerous workshops and weaving classes.*

### Totally Textiles  (Hilary Charlesworth)
Tel: 01730 817191
www.totallytextiles.co.uk
www.theloomexchange.co.uk
*Hilary makes fantastic rugs, hangings and tapestries in her Sussex workshop. She taught me how to spin wool, and made a beautiful rug for Meadowgate. She runs a variety of courses, and her Loom Exchange website sells second-hand spinning, weaving and textile items, and a selection of books.*

## STAINED GLASS
*To find a course or workshop near you, see below and also log onto some of the websites listed under Craft Courses.*

### Abinger Stained Glass  (Amanda Winfield)
Abinger Hammer
Nr Dorking
Surrey RH5 6SH
Tel: 01306 730617
www.abinger-stained-glass.co.uk
*Amanda helped me make a delightful stained-glass light-catcher. She also runs courses.*

### British Society of Master Glass Painters
www.bsmgp.org.uk
*Devoted to preserving and promoting the stained-glass heritage of Britain, this body organises lectures, walks and talks, conferences and exhibitions.*

### Contemporary Glass Society
c/o Broadfield House Glass Museum
Compton Drive
Kingswinford
West Midlands DY6 9NS
Tel: 01379 741120
www.cgs.org.uk
*This website lists exhibitions and events, and also has a gallery that sells a stunning range of work.*

**Creative Glass**
12 Sextant Park
Medway City Estate
Rochester
Kent ME2 4LU
Tel: 01634 735416
www.creativeglassshop.co.uk
*Recommended by Amanda Winfield, this company supplies fusing glass and also runs courses.*

**National Glass Centre**
Liberty Way
Sunderland SR6 0GL
Tel: 0191 515 5555
www.nationalglasscentre.com
*A cultural and educational resource housed (appropriately) in a spectacular glass building. It runs classes in glassblowing and stained glass.*

**Tempsford Stained Glass**
The Old School
Tempsford
Bedfordshire SG19 2AW
Tel: 01767 640235
www.tempsfordstainedglass.co.uk
*Recommended by Amanda Winfield for basic stained-glass supplies.*

**Welsh School of Architectural Glass**
Swansea Metropolitan University
Mount Pleasant
Swansea SA1 6ED
Tel: 01792 481000
www.sihe.ac.uk
*Offers degree courses in the art of stained glass.*

## STENCILLING
*To find a course or workshop near you, see below and also log onto some of the websites listed under Craft Courses.*

**The Stencil Library  (Helen Morris)**
Stocksfield Hall
Stocksfield
Northumberland NE43 7TN

Tel: 01661 844844
www.stencil-library.com
*Helen taught me how to stencil, and made some striking blinds for the TV series. She also runs courses in stencilling.*

## UPHOLSTERY
*To find a course or workshop near you, see below and also log onto some of the websites listed under Craft Courses.*

**Guild of Traditional Upholsterers**
www.gtu.org.uk
*This organisation aims to promote the craft of traditional handmade upholstery, and to protect both the customer and the future of the craft. Its website contains a list of qualified upholsterers around the UK.*

**Fraser McKay**
7 Bridge Barns
Long Sutton
Langport
Somerset TQ10 9PZ
Tel: 01458 241662
www.mckay-upholstery.co.uk
*Fraser taught me the principles of upholstery and restored beauty to my Georgian chair. His website shows the process of reupholstering various items.*

## WALLPAPER
*The following individuals and companies produce very special wallpapers. Some of them will also help you to design your own wallpaper and then print it for you. If you're interested in the wallpaper I made in the TV series, see Emma Molony's entry in the Screen-printing section.*

**Cole & Son**
Lifford House
199 Eade Road
London N4 1DN
Tel: 020 8442 8844
www.cole-and-son.com
*A prime source for authentic period wallpapers.*

**Hatley Print**
29 Shand Street
London SE1 2ES
Tel: 020 7403 4410
www.hatleyprint.co.uk
*This company makes short runs of bespoke handmade wallpaper.*

**The Shop Floor Project**
Tel: 01229 715154
www.theshopfloorproject.com
*This site features handmade wallpaper by a changing selection of talented designers.*

**Bernard Thorp**
53 Chelsea Manor Street
London SW3 5RZ
Tel: 020 7352 1022)
www.bernardthorp.co.uk
*A leading designer of bespoke fabrics and wall coverings.*

**University of the Arts London**
272 High Holborn
London WC1V 7EY
Tel: 020 7514 6000
www.arts.ac.uk
*Runs courses in surface design, which includes textiles and wallpaper.*

**Erica Wakerley**
Studio 5
96 De Beauvoir Road
London N1 4EN
Tel: 07940 577620
www.printpattern.com
*This designer produces a range of innovative wallpapers.*

## WILLOW-WORKING

*To find a course or workshop near you, see below and also log onto some of the websites listed under Craft Courses.*

**Basket Makers Association**
www.basketassoc.org
*Here you can find a list of craftspeople who specialise in basket-making, willow-working and chair seating. It also includes a list of those who run courses.*

**Richard & Sue Kerwood**
Windrush Willow
Higher Barn
Sidmouth Road
Aylesbeare
Exeter
Devon EX5 2JJ
Tel: 01395 233669
www.windrushwillow.com
*Richard and Sue grow and weave 105 different types of willow. They also run courses at various venues around the UK.*

## KIRSTIE'S HOMEMADE HOME

www.channel4.com/4homes/on-tv/kirstie-s-homemade-home
*Visit this terrific website for lots of information about the TV series and all the crafts it features.*

## KIRSTIE ALLSOPP

www.movingsense.co.uk
*This website contains information about Meadowgate, and also lists craftspeople that Kirstie has met on her travels.*

# INDEX

# KIRSTIE'S ACKNOWLEDGEMENTS

Few books are as much a group effort as this one, partly because it is a book about a house, a television show and the efforts of numerous talented, dedicated people. In the beginning there was Will, with whom Ben and I bought Meadowgate, and Chris Ottewell at Barclays, who lent us the money. Then there was Adrian Harris, who loves Meadowgate as much as we do, and Ross Board and his team at Dev Build in Axminster, who brought the house back to life. Then there was Chrissie Fearnehough and her team – no one makes curtains quicker or better, and the brilliant Clemmie Hambro, who despite being heavily pregnant, laboured in the garden for days. Many thanks are also due to the stylist Sasha Schwerdt, who left behind her animals and learnt to email in order to bring the vision together, add her magic and keep everyone sane! Thanks also to Sasha's daughter Eloise, who worked alongside her, and to Elanor Holland and Helen Knight. Then came the TV folk… I am hugely grateful to everyone at IWC who made such a lovely show, led by Hamish Barbour with whom I have worked for so long, and including Sarah Walmsley, Eileen Herlihy, Nina Brown, Chrissie Butler, Lisa McCann, Jeannot Hutcheson, Julia Bird, Ellie De Court, Lorraine McKechnie, Laura Wiseman, Alex McCarter, Ale D'Avanzo, Gail Hamilton, Martyn Bon, Helen Moore, Luble Scrivens, Andrew Walmsley and Jane Muirhead. I am also very grateful to Andrew Jackson, Walter Iuzzolino and Sue Murphy at Channel 4, who believed I could transfer my passion for crafts and all things battered and bruised to the screen. You have *all* brought crafts back to television. And, of course, thanks to Hannah Warren, who let us have the money to do it.

Throughout my career in TV I have been guided by Anne Sweetbaum at Arlington Enterprises, and by Suzanne and Hilary, to whom I owe many thanks. Then there were the craftspeople who agreed to be part of this madness and so generously gave their time and energy and never held back from handing over the tricks of their trade; who continued to do their thing despite being asked to do it ten times over, and 'slower for the camera', and who were so patient with me. A big thank you to them all, and extra thanks to those who also feature in this book: Emma Biggs (mosaic), Judith Blacklock (flower arranging), David Constable (candles), Jenny Elesmore (soap), Eileen Garsed (lampshade), Elanor Holland (lavender bag, doorstop, pinboard, napkin folding), Penny Horne (shrunken jumper cosies, découpage), Suzie Johnson (knitting), Erika Knight (crochet), Christine McInnes (gilding), Fraser McKay (upholstery), Emma Molony (screen-printing), Helen Morris (stencilling), Debbie Siniska (rag rag), Mich Turner (cake decorating). At the time of writing we're in the midst of filming series two, so I would like to thank *all* the craftspeople and the families who let us into their homes.

Just at the point when I thought I could take a breather, some clever clogs thought it was a good idea to do a book. But I am very grateful to everyone at Hodder, including Nicky Ross, Trish Burgess, Zelda Turner, Sarah Hammond and the team. Thanks to Mark Lesbirel and Victoria Ramirez at RDF Rights, to the brilliant and inspiring Emma and Alex at Smith & Gilmour, who designed this lovely book, and to Chris Terry, who took many of the pictures.

It would be entirely unfair to get through this book without acknowledging just how much I learnt during my time on *Country Living Magazine*. I credit people like Francine Lawrence, my editor, and Vicky Carlisle, the features editor in my day, with introducing me to so much that was new in the field of British crafts. Working on the first few Country Living Fairs was brilliant fun – it was there that I met some wonderful potters and I began to buy the mugs, jugs, teapots and bowls that now fill our home.

Finally, I have to say a very special thank you to our friends and neighbours in Welcombe, especially everyone at The Old Smithy Inn who kept us going, to Phil Spencer, who put up with my infidelity, to Sarah Walmsley, who is the best boss ever, to Lisa McCann, who is practically perfect in every way, to my parents, who are an inspiration, to the home team of Heather, Maravic, Angelina, Katharine and Chris, Sophie and Catherine who make it all possible, to my in-laws Gretchen and Viv Andersen at the Lacquer Chest, who gave us so many lovely bits for the house, and most of all to Ben, who teaches me something every day and who never wavers in his optimism and love.

This book is published to accompany the television series *Kirstie's Homemade Home*, an IWC Media production for Channel 4, © IWC Media Limited MMIX.
www.iwcmedia.co.uk

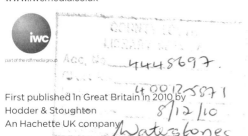

First published in Great Britain in 2010 by
Hodder & Stoughton
An Hachette UK company

1

Commissioning editor: Zelda Turner
Project editor: Patricia Burgess
Step-by-step illustrations: Kuo Kang Chen
Embroidery illustrations: Louise Gardiner
Photography styling: Sasha Schwerdt
Design and art direction by Smith & Gilmour, London

Typeset in American Typewriter and Gotham
Printed and bound by Graphicom s.r.l.

Hodder & Stoughton policy is to use papers that are natural, renewable and recyclable products and made from wood grown in sustainable forests. The logging and manufacturing processes are expected to conform to the environmental regulations of the country of origin.

Hodder & Stoughton Ltd
338 Euston Road
London NW1 3BH
www.hodder.co.uk

## Publisher's acknowledgements

The publisher would like to thank the following people for providing items for the photo shoots:
**Baileys Home & Garden** – Kilner jar lights (page 28) and wooden bath rack (page 61)
**Helen Knight** – mirror (page 61, right)
**Lawrence's Auction House, Crewkerne** – Georgian glass bottles (page 63)
**Will Shakspeare** – glassware (pages 6/7, 90/91)
Thanks also to:
**Sophie Fox** for testing all the projects.

**Meadowgate** is a holiday house shared by two families, and when not being used by us, it is rented out. For more information visit www.movingsense.co.uk

**Reward...** In this book you will see many shots of my red ring (page 98, for example), which I lost on the day we did mosaics. There is a £1000 reward for its return. Learn more at www.kirstieslostring.co.uk